The Fifth Disciple

Choose Again and Find True Happiness

The Fifth Disciple

Choose Again and Find True Happiness

Cynthia Bové

BOOKS

Winchester, UK
Washington, USA

First published by O-Books, 2011
O-Books is an imprint of John Hunt Publishing Ltd., Laurel House, Station Approach,
Alresford, Hants, SO24 9JH, UK
office1@o-books.net
www.o-books.com

For distributor details and how to order please visit the 'Ordering' section on our website.

Text copyright: Cynthia Bové 2009

ISBN: 978 1 84694 420 8

A CIP catalogue record for this book is available from the British Library.

Design: Stuart Davies

COVER: Hubble NGC 6397 Star Cluster Photo. Spaceimages.com

Comments are welcome! www cdbove@aol.com

Portions from *'Your Immortal Reality'*, Gary R. Renard, copyright 2006; and
'Disappearance of the Universe', Gary R. Renard, copyright 2002, 2003, 2004
are reprinted by permission of Hay House, Inc., Carlsbad, CA

Printed in the UK by CPI Antony Rowe
Printed in the USA by Offset Paperback Mfrs, Inc

We operate a distinctive and ethical publishing philosophy in all
areas of our business, from our global network of authors to
production and worldwide distribution.

CONTENTS

Footnote References / Book Abbreviations

W= Workbook, *A Course in Miracles*

T= Text, *A Course in Miracles*

M= Manual for Teachers, *A Course in Miracles*

DU= *Disappearance of the Universe*

YIR= *Your Immortal Reality*

PGT= *Pursah's Gospel of Thomas*

G-I= *Glossary-Index for A Course in Miracles*

SP= *Song of Prayer*

A Course in Miracles footnote references are arranged as follows:
The letters indicate the section of the book, and the numerals indicate page number, paragraph and line number, respectively.

For Example:
(W [workbook] 456 [page] 7 [paragraph] 8 [line])

In the Old and New Testaments, the book is referenced, then chapter, then verse.
If the reference does not have numbered paragraphs or lines, only the page number is indicated.

PART 1

Prelude

We have taken several profound spiritual texts and drawn a number of parallels between them, and combined these ideas to gain a broader understanding of our life's purpose, and to help us navigate the unpredictable roads of our life's journey. We will find that each of the documents discussed will impart understanding to the other and will give us insights that can unlock mysteries which have been concealed from mankind's awareness for generations. We will be specifically looking at a rendition of *The Gospel of Thomas* and *A Course in Miracles*.

The *Course's* edicts, reinforced by the contemporary perspective of *The Gospel of Thomas*, can point us in a new direction and reveal new options that will lead to a thought reversal as to what we consider real and important. We are encouraged to travel with a different guide than we have in the past, One who will smooth our way and make straight our path.

We have found *A Course in Miracles* to be a distinctive manuscript that exposes the reader to a different way of viewing life. It imparts the unique understanding that there is a way out of the current perceptual prison of a suffering world.

We will learn that we have an alternate choice as to how we perceive and think about the world, and that choice provides us with a map and a compass that can lead us back to the Home that we have never left. We will find that we have put our faith in a thought system that has repeatedly betrayed us, and guidelines are now available that can transfigure everything that we perceive. We are given keys that will assist us to see beyond form to the formless, and unite with the flawless Vision that sees our True Self as It really is. Although the *Course* is Christian in its language and venue, it supersedes the parameters of any one doctrine as it confronts and discusses universal spiritual themes.

The Gospel of Thomas is a written collection of Jesus' parables, many of which are found in the New Testament. An entire intact copy of this gospel was unearthed over sixty years ago, but the average person knows little to nothing about it. These Sayings convey the Love of our Father that Jesus continually exemplified. As we consider the passages from this treatise, we can gain further insights into the life and times of Jesus and the disciples, and we will be able to apply that wisdom to our lives. We have included this revised gospel in a subsequent chapter, and will presently give an account of how the original document was found.

These books studied side by side will open up a window into the past so that we can catch a glimmer of the spirit and message of the Master. We will move from a literal understanding of these teachings to a more spiritual comprehension of the underlying meanings that might not have been so obvious at first. They will offer us a clear path to follow and if we choose to, we can place our footprints in His own.

Let us now open our hearts and minds and hear with our inner ear the miracle of these teachings that lead us ever forward to remember God in all of His Splendor and Love.

Chapter One

Origins

Let us first look at *The Gospel of Thomas* and explore its origins. *The Gospel of Thomas* is a collection of Sayings that is claimed to have been written by one of the twelve disciples of Jesus. This complete text, among others, was discovered in the desert of Upper Egypt near Nag-Hammadi in 1945.

The early church fathers, notably Origen of Alexandria and Hyppolytus[1] were aware of *The Gospel of Thomas* and mentioned this gospel in a few contexts, albeit in a negative manner. Up until this point though, most of the writings by this disciple were thought to have been lost or destroyed during the early Church's struggle to define scripture and unify it into a consistent doctrine. From a scattering of a few existing remnants, scholars had only been able to assemble a sketchy picture of what Thomas had written.

What little that was known of this gospel had always been regarded by the Christian Church with skepticism as it was considered to be a heretical text, Gnostic in nature and running contrary to canonical scripture.

There is an age-old dispute between the teachings of Gnosticism and those of Christianity. The reason for that debate not only has to do with the radically different foundational premise of Gnosticism, but also their view of Jesus. They considered Jesus to be sent as a liberator of mankind, and through gnosis (knowledge) he would free man from an inherently evil world, so that at death man could reunite with the Supreme God. This runs contrary to the Christian view of Jesus as the savior of mankind and who, as God incarnate, sacrificed his body to take up the burden of mankind's sins.

We can see how different these views of Jesus and the world are and will not be debating these topics here. What we will be doing is using the Sayings from *The Gospel of Thomas* to impart a different perspective on a number of spiritual themes.

Thomas' Gospel was discovered by chance as an Arab peasant was searching for an indigenous fertilizer in the arid desert of his homeland. In his travels he stumbled upon an earthenware jar and broke it open. To his surprise he found that it contained more than a dozen fourth-century papyrus codices and manuscripts bound in leather. These codices consisted of fifty-two texts written in the Coptic[2] language. This collection of documents was later named *The Nag Hammadi Library,* or *The Coptic Gnostic Library,* and among those ancient tractates was a collection of Sayings called *The Gospel of Thomas.*

This text had not been viewed in its entirety for centuries. One can imagine the disruption within the Christian community when this complete ancient text of *The Gospel of Thomas* was found after having been buried for over 1,600 years. (It had been in circulation for about 400 years before it was buried.)

Was there now a possibility that a long closed door might open and this new information could be studied or additional perspectives be embraced? Could some contemporary theories unsettle the streamlined, traditionally accepted doctrine? Could the Church's foundational doctrine and belief system perhaps change or be supplemented to be objectively discussed and evaluated? It does not appear to be happening anytime soon, and we will look a few possible reasons why this is the case.

An additional discovery that has added to this small but growing cornucopia of information about *The Gospel of Thomas* was a heretofore uncertain correlation between this gospel's Coptic version and older Greek fragments called the Oxyrhynchus fragments. These fragments were unearthed years before *The Gospel of Thomas,* and were found in 1897-1903 during an excavation of an ancient library in Oxyrhynchus, Egypt. It had been speculated that there were remnants of *The Gospel of Thomas* among the thousands of fragments of Biblical script found in this library, and the later 1945 Coptic discovery confirmed this supposition.

These early fragments posed some thought-provoking ramifications. Our first consideration is that these fragments establish that the Coptic version is a later translation from an earlier text, and it was also translated from another language. Secondarily, as the Greek Oxyrhynchus version predates this Coptic translation, it gives this gospel historical verification and legitimacy. Additionally, this Greek version has been dated at 130-250 A.D., so not only was it written around the time of the canonical gospels, but a surprising possibility emerges that *The Gospel of Thomas* may have even preceded them (See Appendix A).

Even with this information, Christian theologians to this day dispute the legitimacy of *The Gospel of Thomas* and dismiss it as a heretical Gnostic text. As we objectively review *The Gospel of Thomas* we will find that about half of the gospel has direct parallels to the canonical gospels, and much of the rest of can be linked theologically to the New Testament. However, even with this information, *The Gospel of Thomas* is still generally ignored and remains obscure.

As we investigate the first lines of this unearthed gospel, we find the quote, 'Whosoever discovers the hidden interpretations of these sayings will not taste death'. This quote that is found frequently throughout the gospel may be one of the reasons that this text has been considered to be a Gnostic document.

One of the precepts that defined Gnosticism is that initiates believed that only they had the understanding and secret knowledge of what Jesus really meant in his discourses. However, using the word 'secret' does not automatically turn this gospel into a Gnostic text. A case in point would be the Gospel of Mark, where Jesus tells the disciples that the secret of the Kingdom of God belongs to them, and it is outsiders that receive everything in parables[3]. Further, in the same gospel we read that Jesus explained the meaning of his parables to the disciples in private[4]. These Biblical quotes show that *Thomas' Gospel* should not be regarded as a Gnostic teaching based on a phrase that has 'secret' in it or if certain teachings were relayed to a select group.

As we look anew at this first Saying in *The Gospel of Thomas* and progress in the studies of our additional materials, the possibility of another interpretation arises. It may well mean that we 'will never taste death' if we begin to focus on removing the obstacles that hinder us from understanding that we are one with our Father in Spirit. By changing our perspectives we will attain a spiritual resurrection and a transformation of our minds.

We are familiar with the New Testament gospels written by the disciples Matthew, Mark, Luke and John and now because of the Nag Hammadi discovery, we find that we can supplement our understanding of them with Thomas' recorded dialogue. As we review this 'fifth' gospel and realize that it stands on its own merit, (even as it reflects the teachings from the other four gospels) we will discover that it offers added insights into the thoughts of Jesus and of the times in which he lived.

We may find with this complementary gospel in hand, that Jesus is entreating us to look deeper into the hidden or metaphysical interpretations that may not be so obvious at first. It would impart a sense of freedom to know that as we follow his guidance he will teach us to listen within to the still, quiet voice of Truth and hear His Answer for ourselves. We will discover that this text written by Thomas, complemented by our other spiritual resources conveys a concise message of wisdom that is relevant to our lives and will help us to navigate this chaotic world.

After much consideration, we have chosen to use a unique translation of *The Gospel of Thomas* and have included it in its entirety in a subsequent section. This gospel is named *Pursah's Gospel of Thomas*[5] and is a modified version of the Nag Hammadi text. As we will see, it streamlines the text to reveal a consistent and unified message. If desired, one can also compare these Sayings with the Nag Hammadi text to make further comparisons. One will still find that the contemporary messages discussed can be applied to all translated versions of this gospel.

Since we have focused on a document that has been revised, an immediate question one would wonder is; how could an ancient text be modified, and who would have the authority to alter any part of *The Gospel of Thomas*, which after 1,600 years of anonymity has come to us as part of *The Nag Hammadi Library*?

This is a good question, and will be answered shortly. We will come to appreciate the reasons why this modified rendition of *The Gospel of Thomas* was chosen to relay the enduring messages from Jesus.

The Introduction of Pursah

Let us look at the narrative that introduces Pursah and reveals her interesting part in relaying *The Gospel of Thomas*. One day in 1992, to the surprise of Gary Renard[6], a mysterious couple appeared from out of nowhere and introduced themselves as the ascended masters, Arten and Pursah. (Ascended masters are beings who have transcended the bounds of human limitations.) Their mission was to reveal the miraculous powers of advanced forgiveness that could change our perception of the world. Their insights were coherent, integrated, and relayed a unified message of love.

Among the many subjects discussed with Arten and Pursah, one unexpected topic was the disclosure of their past. Arten revealed that at the time of Jesus he was one of the twelve disciples named Thaddeus, also known as Jude. Pursah was the disciple Thomas, and had complete recall of that life, hence enabling her to alter the Nag Hammadi version of *Thomas' Gospel* for accuracy. We have used the maxim 'fifth disciple' to refer to Thomas, because we have found that this document lends support to the four traditionally accepted gospels and expands our knowledge of the thoughts of the Master.

This unusual introduction to the fifth disciple can lead us to a question about the subject of reincarnation. We may ask, what is reincarnation exactly? The premise of reincarnation is that one has lived before in a body and will live once more. It further states that when all of our thoughts and deeds have been balanced and we have come into alignment with God's Will, we will no longer need to return to earth, but will once again be in our Father's Presence for all time. It is difficult to come to a specific conclusion about reincarnation since it is a personal belief based on ones own experiences.

However, in reference to these documents, the import of this question recedes as we look to the text of *The Gospel of Thomas* and ask ourselves if this revised manuscript provides a consistent and unified message? Do we find that the majority of the significant Logia remain the same as the Nag Hammadi version? Is this gospel more logical in its new format? If our answers are affirmative, we can move on to study the deeper meanings of the Sayings, and endeavor to embrace the eternal Oneness that they advocate.

As we examine *The Gospel of Thomas,* it is a poignant prospect to sit once again at the feet of the Master, to listen to his words and thoughts and to look with him into the heart of the parables.

As was already mentioned, to complement our understanding of *Thomas' Gospel* and to gain a fuller picture of our life's purpose, the major metaphysical philosophy that we will discuss in depth is *A Course in Miracles*. These teachings can be used to enhance our awareness of a Reality beyond this physical world. The *Course* is a unique spiritual text that speaks of mans' creation, why we are here and what we need to do to get back to our true Reality. It speaks of fear and redemption, of the ego and the Holy Spirit and how we are part of God's Oneness that has no beginning or end. The *Course* helps us unfold the treasure map of our salvation, and as we apply the tenets outlined therein to our lives we will rediscover the Will of God for our lives and learn what we need to do to fulfill our destiny. Throughout its pages we will come to witness the transformative power of accepting our Oneness with our Father, even as we become aware of the reasons for its delay. Our objective is to use the methods outlined by the *Course* to liberate our minds and change our thinking so that we can remove the blocks to our true vision. As we tap into the Universal One Mind, we will be able to see beyond the body to the Spirit that eternally dwells in the Reality of our indisputable Oneness.

We will now review some of the foundational teachings from *A Course in Miracles* to complement our understanding of the underlying message found in the revised edition of *The Gospel of Thomas*.

Chapter Two

A Course in Miracles

As the teachings of *A Course in Miracles* unfold, we will study some profound insights that reveal a philosophy unparalleled in spiritual thought. It is an extraordinary self-study course, with timeless teachings that have no religious affiliation, even though there are biblical references and language. It is an original system of thought that puts us in touch with our real Mind, and by so doing, peace, joy, and healing follow naturally. As these teachings are embraced, and one accepts the thought system of advanced forgiveness and Love that are outlined, our awareness will be transformed and we will move forward to an inner peace and true strength that is a gift of untold proportions.

Within the outline of *A Course in Miracles* we will discover many keys that will help us to find the happiness that we seek even as we reside within a perpetually sorrowful world. If applied with diligence and focus, these keys have the ability to catapult our thinking into alignment with God's Will for our lives. That Will has never altered and has never varied, it has only been unrecognized.

One of the first things that we will notice about the *Course's* language is that it is presented in a Christian context. It uses the masculine form when referring to God, the One Son, the Holy Spirit and our fellow human beings. This format was certainly not meant to offend anyone, but was chosen to embrace, not exclude those in the Western Judeo-Christian culture who are familiar with this type of language, and so we have adopted it into our format as well.

To understand the humble truths that *A Course in Miracles* can bring to our awareness, we will also need to examine the subtle timbre of the *Course's* language. We will look at some terms which are used that do not have the same meanings that we normally ascribe to them, and for clarity, we have devoted certain sections to discuss those and other relevant topics.

For one, we will take a look at the meaning of forgiveness. When we use the word 'advanced' forgiveness, we are speaking of a forgiveness that ultimately sees the purity of the Son of God dwelling in Spirit beyond the body and form, where there is no error. In conventional forgiveness, one first sees the error and *then* tries to overlook it and forgive it. As we understand the new meanings outlined by the *Course* and apply those precepts to our lives, we will begin to appreciate the benefits of changing our mind as to how we view our brother. We will come to understand the reasons for our current outlooks and why the changing our mind is an essential ingredient to progressing on our spiritual journey. As we begin to forgive him for his mistakes, we will introduce into our consciousness the forgiveness of ourselves. As we dismantle the obstacles that we have set up between ourselves, our brother and our Creator, we will make contact with the Self that has always been, and begin to reweave the tapestry of God's Wholeness back into our awareness.

We will also methodically examine a number of terms that relate to the unconditional love that our Father has for us, as well as terms that relate to the blocks that hinder us from experiencing that love. We may personally define love as an exclusive love relationship or the love of a parent for their child. The *Course's* definition of love actually expands beyond any and all limiting definitions, and is regarded as the all-encompassing Love of the Father for every part of Himself that excludes no one or no thing. So when we are asked to choose Love, this does not mean the love found in the world. The world promotes special love, and that love rejects some and accepts others. We are speaking of the complete, all-inclusive Love of the Father for *all* of His children. This is the Love that is not necessarily physical, but sees beyond form to the indwelling essence of Spirit, and cannot and does not exclude anyone. As we choose to Love as He Loves, we are then enfolded into the Thoughts of our Creator Who sees us *and* our brother as eternally One with Him. Truth, peace, and forgiveness are a few of the synonyms that are used in the *Course* to touch upon these aspects of the Divine. We will find that all of the references to the Love of God are related to this foundational thought of unified Oneness.

Let us now consider some pivotal terms used throughout *A Course in Miracles*. We will look at the expression 'Son of God' or the 'One Son'. These terms are used to refer to the Christic image that resides within us all as the One Son and issue of Our Father. This idea enhances our metaphysical understanding of who we are beyond form, and is not related to any one doctrine and can be applied to any spiritual path.

This expression of the 'One Son' is regarded to be the unified Presence of which we all are a part and has existed before anything that was made. The integrated One Son is an indissoluble part of the essence of the silent breath before the Word came forth and is comprised of everything after the Word came forth. It is an element of the unchangeableness of eternity that Is, and is where we all are dwelling in the eternal Present, *now*. We are reminded of a passage in the Bible about our creation; 'The Spirit of God hath made me, and the breath of the Almighty hath given me life.'[1] This becomes only a glimmer of what we truly are beyond the vagaries of time.

The 'One Son' has dreamed of fragmentation but his Spirit is still part of the Whole and he has only forgotten that this is so. Thus, this expression transcends time and space and refers not only to Jesus, but to all of God's children, male *and* female who are all a part of the Whole. Jesus is nonetheless the definitive personification of the One Son. He understood that, 'he was in the Father and the Father was in him...'[2] He demonstrated this knowledge to the world and was the beacon of light that came to guide us Home. Our potential is to be as he is, and as he himself has said in the New Testament 'Verily, Verily, I say unto you, he that believeth on me the works that I do shall he do also; and greater works than these shall he do...'[3] Our gratitude knows no bounds as we realize that our loving Guide has come again to reveal to us the message of our Divinity and guide us back to our Place of Origin where we will reside with him in timelessness.

Nevertheless, 'Child of God' can be substituted by the reader, or any other term that feels comfortable, until the words themselves are transcended and their underlying message and meaning are recognized. What is important, over and above the semantics of the biblical expression, is the realization that the term 'Son of God' represents *us* as the One Son, beyond time and space, forever united in the Mind and Spirit of our Father. This is the Mind that the *Course* addresses, not the 'us' that we identify with as individual bodies.

This clears up any confusion that may happen when statements are made in the *Course* that could be interpreted to mean that an individual can save the world, or it is a person's holiness that blesses the world. What we are is united together in Spirit and our fundamental nature is beyond any appearance or manifestation. Our essence that is ultimately One with our Father pervades everything so thoroughly that it becomes an ethereal thought that not only penetrates the space between the electrons of the atoms but simultaneously soars in all directions and into all dimensions.

Even though this is the nature of our being, we have lost touch with it and are unaware of this connective force that is our very life. So now our individual dramas play out upon the world, our loves and hates and our choices for good or ill, all the while the Reality of who we are beyond form has been forgotten.

This brings to mind images of turbulent waves tossing and churning above changeless silent depths, and the tranquil water beneath the turbulence is totally unaffected by what is transpiring above. Our focus has been upon the chaotic surface of the water while unbeknownst to us the calm unchanging water of the depths has always supported our existence.

If we have a small willingness to acknowledge that there may be another way to see the world, then the door will swing open and all things shall become clear. When we let the Holy Spirit into our lives with the little willingness to find a better way, we will have a companion Who will joyfully accompany us for the rest of our journey Home.

A Short Study in Duality
We are told that deep within the mind of the One Son, on a metaphysical level where there is no duality (subject and object), everything as we know it is actually enveloped in the One Mind of God, and there *is* nothing else. The *Course* gently directs us in how to *recover* this understanding of our Oneness with all life; it is done by methodically removing the blocks that we have unwittingly placed between ourselves and that forgotten knowledge. Since we now believe that we are a product of a dualistic environment, we are gently led to see the truth of our dualistic thoughts by seeing the logic of contrasts.

From the perspective of the *Course*, an important study in contrasts and duality is the ego, and we will soon look at it more thoroughly. Here, the term 'ego' represents the 'wrong minded thought system', and it is this mode of thinking that we want to extricate ourselves from as it only leads to our suffering and despair. The ego's thought system is the author of the world of perception, of time and change, of beginnings and endings and it is the world which we have embraced as our reality. We may be surprised to hear that the whole of the ego's interpretive world is the complete antithesis to the Realm of God. It has no part of the changelessness and totality of the Unified Realm that has no beginning or end.

This idea of the completely unified, changeless Mind of God

has a lot in common with a spiritual philosophy called non-dualism. This study is centered on the thought that we / everything are One, and that there *are* no differences between us because we are made in our Father's image and likeness which is Spirit.

A beautiful rendition of the idea of Oneness is depicted in the Workbook and unconditionally describes this thought of non-dualism:

'Oneness is simply the idea God is. And in His Being, He encompasses all things. No mind holds anything but Him. We say 'God is,' and then we cease to speak, for in that knowledge words are meaningless. There are no lips to speak them and no part of mind sufficiently distinct to feel that it is now aware of something not itself. It has united with its Source. And like its Source Itself, it merely is.'[3A]

The 'right minded' thought system in the *Course* is represented by the Holy Spirit, and there are similarities to many of the ideas of non-dualism. The difference is that even though this 'right minded' thought system is in itself completely unified and contains no negative facets, the Holy Spirit is the aspect of God that knows both thought systems, and provides the One Answer that will show us the way out of our perceptual limitations. His Gentle Voice mediates between the world of perception, which we believe is real, and the realm of knowledge, where no thought exists apart from God. This Unified Realm is where we are as the One Son, now. The Holy Spirit will help us to remember that this is where we have always existed, joined as One Mind and with One Will, and our divine Helper will help us to see and remove the blocks to this knowledge. Our reliance and belief in the vaporous ego world will then dissipate, leaving only the Truth in its place.

As we study in earnest, we will recognize that we have a spiritual mind and that we can reverse our thoughts to those of the Holy Spirit's right minded thinking. We do so by consistently identifying and exposing the ego's defensive thought system for what it is, and then come to realize that we no longer want it. As we are continually shown throughout the *Course* the contrasts between these two thought systems, we can embark upon the path of knowledge that will show us how to unlearn the mistakes of our thinking. We will be provided with the tools that will help us to shed the obstacles that have impeded us from merging with our real Self.

An enlightened Indian sage, Sri Nisargadatta Maharaj[4], illuminated this somewhat confusing idea about the two differing aspects of the self within the individual. He distinguished between them by calling them the 'false self' and the 'I am' (The *Course* would refer to them as the ego and the Holy Spirit). A student did not understand the difference between these two selves, and perhaps thinking them more or less the same, asked 'How or why would the self want to eliminate the self or, put another way, why would one want to use metaphysical acrobatics to make the acrobat disappear?'

Nisargadatta's answer was in accord with some of the ideas that we have been discussing. He said that once a person has a sincere longing for reality, the determination to be free from the false is set in place. When all of the (ego) thoughts of 'I do', 'I feel', and 'I think'(which belong to the 'separate identity') disappear from the field of consciousness, then only what is real is left. This meeting ground is difficult to find if the false self is denied or looked upon with contempt.

When the 'higher Self' (as the independent observer) looks upon the little self with a loving understanding, then that small self is no longer denied but gently released as being unreal and having no substance. The little self will now subsume into the One Self, and the duality of 'I' and 'that' will merge (The *Course* would say that the ego thoughts fade away leaving only the True Self). Now the Higher Self takes charge and becomes the guiding principle of our every thought. It is then that our view of life becomes all-encompassing and far reaching and we see things as they truly are.

The bottom line is that change can only come about if we are willing to look upon all parts of ourselves with compassion and understanding, even those aspects that we most dislike. When we do not deny them but view them as opportunities for growth, then they will fade away to let the light that is true shine forth.

A fundamental key to our freedom is to realize that we *have* a choice, and that we are not imprisoned by one limited thought construct. As our vision expands and we apply the *Course's* precepts and Workbook lessons to our lives, we find to our delight, a panoramic view of peace, joy and security opening up to our sight.

This happy vision of the 'real world' is defined in the *Course* as a peaceful state of mind where our outlooks and interpretations about what we view in the world are changed, and we see all from the Holy Spirit's perspective. We look upon all things with the eyes of Peace, for our minds are permanently healed of the separation thought.

A story will unfold in Chapter Four that explains this separation thought and reveals the reasons why we find ourselves in our present predicament.

Our Spiritual Image

To gain a greater understanding of our motivations and dualistic thought processes, we will find that *A Course in Miracles* candidly describes how we observe this universe. We perceive everything as characterized by duality in a world of comparisons. There is not tall without short, or black without white and as these comparisons exist, so do our judgments. While those judgments are in place we are immersed in the idea of competition with winners and losers, inferiority and superiority and the complexity of competing problems ad infinitum. This concept of duality is converted into an idea about our reality and the world. We see ourselves as a subject with objects external to us and that perception expands to include the entire universe as being outside of us.

With the aid of the *Course* and Jesus at our side, our aim is to change this perception of duality and return to an awareness of the original thought in the Mind of Oneness before the idea of division and separation came into play. We will be able to once again discern the Truth that we had only forgotten, and uncover the veiled answers that we have always sought.

The image of God in which we were created is Spirit and not matter. This idea is our first step in mentally disengaging from the self-importance and specialness that we have harbored about our individual lives. We will find that the import of the physical fades as we contemplate the majesty that resides within.

Let us consider the following quote from the *Course*, where we are reminded that God is Spirit, and the stuff that the world is made of is not within His Awareness.

'What God did not create does not exist. And everything that does exist exists as He created it. The world you see has nothing to do with reality. It is of your own making, and it does not exist.'[5]

Since we have so long identified with our individuality and separateness, it may be a new idea to consider who and what we are beyond the boundaries that we have set up, and to start to grapple with the thought of transcending those limits. What will give clarity to these thoughts is the version of our ontological ('separation') story that is in an upcoming chapter that helps us to understand the nature of this world, as well as understanding why and how deeply we sleep. As we look at these ideas we will gain further insights as to why we see and place so much emphasis on the physical realm as well as the thoughts we have about the part God plays in it.

We can also give these new thoughts some credence as we recognize that God is not a physical presence but a Spiritual Image that we are patterned after, and therefore our Father could only be a Pure Undivided Thought in which duality and separation have no place.

We are reminded in the following excerpt that our creation in Holiness is beyond form and if we do not understand our origins we are cast into uncertainty and doubt as to who we really are.

'What is the Word of God? 'My Son is pure and holy as Myself.' And thus did God become the Father of the Son He loves, for thus was he created...Deny we were created in His Love and we deny our Self, to be unsure of Who we are, and Who our Father is...'[6]

If this knowledge of our Divine Reality is obscured by identifying ourselves with the physical world of attack and division, we believe that we are something that we are not. We become lost in a state of forgetfulness and vain imaginings. We despair of any hope of redemption by believing that our transgressions are indelibly stamped upon us for eternity.

We can waken to our True Self by relying on the Holy Spirit Who reminds us that we now have the opportunity to make another choice, and this time we can choose rightly. As we continually make the choice for the Holy Spirit, it follows that we will begin to remember our Father and we will recall who we are, where we came from and our unity as the One Son. We will recollect:

Christ is God's Son as He created Him. He is the Self we share, uniting us with one another and with God as well. He is the Thought which still abides within the Mind that is His Source...The Holy Spirit reaches from the Christ in you to all your dreams, and bids them come to Him, to be translated into truth.[7]

There is nothing else except our eternal Presence as One in God's spiritual Kingdom. This point of view will change our perception of the world, and bring about a thought reversal as to what we deem real and important.

Of course, these are not the only spiritual teachings that will advance us on our path, and they can be used to supplement any chosen path. But if we endeavor to reverse our thinking about the world and its meaning and take *A Course in Miracles* seriously, we will find that time collapses and we will be propelled faster on the road to enlightenment. That road becomes a venture in simply remembering.

These are intriguing ideas to contemplate, and even as we examine them it is highly recommended to research and review *A Course in Miracles* for further elaborations and an in depth study of these concepts.

Initiation of the Course

A Course in Miracles is an advanced teaching for the New Age, given to us by Jesus through his scribe Helen Schucman and transcribed by her associate Bill Thetford over a period of seven years. She was attuned to Jesus' voice and wrote his message verbatim. Only Jesus' views and terminology are contained within this remarkable three part book, which includes a Text, a Workbook for Students with lessons for every day of the year, and a Manual for Teachers.

Helen Schucman and Bill Thetford were Professors of Medical Psychology at Columbia University's College of Physicians and Surgeons in New York City. Both were immersed in the hustle and bustle of the academic world, and seemed an unlikely pair for this remarkable undertaking. Nevertheless, the fact that they were receptive to find a better and more loving way to live life, demonstrates one can never tell when the time for a miracle is at hand.

Helen Schucman spoke candidly about herself in the preface of *A Course in Miracles;*

I was a…psychologist, educator, conservative in theory and atheistic in belief, I was working in a prestigious and highly academic setting. And then something happened that triggered a chain of events I could never have predicted...I was still very surprised when I wrote, 'This is a course in miracles.' That was my introduction to the Voice. It made no sound, but seemed to be giving me a kind of rapid, inner dictation which I took down in a shorthand notebook. The writing was never automatic. It could be interrupted at any time and later picked up again...It seemed to be a special assignment I had somehow, somewhere agreed to complete.[8]

As she and Bill Thetford had a 'little willingness' to embark on this difficult new venture, Bill settled into the task of typing out what the Voice 'said' from Helen's notes. By so doing, and offering encouragement and support, Helen was able to complete her task.

The *Course* was not edited to suit any religion, nor changed in order to appeal to a generic audience. Its final editing was directed by Jesus through Helen Schucman, and remained unaltered as it was published by the *Foundation for Inner Peace*. In contrast to *The Gospel of Thomas*, it is a complete presentation as well as a comprehensive training.[9]

Throughout this work many tools will be used from the *Course* that point out key concepts and illuminate certain ideas that will give us a fuller picture of our life's purpose. As we explore the spiritual wisdom that the *Course* has to offer in combination with *The Gospel of Thomas* found in Part 2, we will not only see the thread of Oneness that is woven throughout the Sayings but we will find that these materials have the ability to transform our mind about the nature of reality.

With our combination of sources, we are endeavoring to provide a fuller picture of the Master's thoughts and ideas and how we can more fully understand those keys and apply them to our lives. As we correlate past and present materials for our review, it will help us navigate the treacherous waters of the ego thought system and come to a recognition of our True Self.

Chapter Three

The Ego

To gain an understanding of the subtleties of these teachings, it is important to mention that when we speak of the ego and its thought system, we are always referring to the original thought of separation and fear. We are not speaking of the ego of traditional psychology which is described as the inter-relationship of the ego, the id and the superego. The formal psychology of the world identifies the ego as mediating between the internal psyche of a person and their external reality, whereas *A Course in Miracles* defines the ego as an illusory self that has been embraced as real. Jesus summarizes the ego as follows, it is;

> 'but a dream of what you really are. A thought you are apart from your Creator and a wish to be what He created not... (it is also identifying oneself as) the brotherless illusion and the self that seem(s) alone in all the universe.'[1]

This ego mindset of the world gives us the sense of being adrift and alone. We had thought this ego world was our only reality, and it is no wonder that we would seek here for answers. Our problems result from having forgotten our Source which is our only true Reality and lies beyond this world and its mechanizations. Only the Truth that is outside the dream can shine away the shadows and provide the one true Answer.

We have to admit that searching in the world for answers to the world's problems has been frustrating and the solutions that we have tried to implement have been ineffective or temporary. We have never found permanent solutions to our difficulties, because the reality of the problem itself has never been questioned. We must realize that one cannot heal an illusion with an illusion.

We will look at this thought provoking idea soon, but for now let us try to overcome our apprehension of confronting our subliminal fears and misperceptions by asking for the guidance of Jesus and the Holy Spirit. The way to recognize our hidden fears for what they are is to honestly look at our actions without criticism or judgment, and understand that they are just a product of the ego thought system that has nothing to do with our Real Self. We will then start to take responsibility for the choices that we have made in the past, and begin to make new choices without guilt in the present. The mistakes that were taken so seriously will fall away and the One Answer that solves all difficulties will be disclosed.

One of the main themes of the *Course* that runs contrary to the ego mindset is the mind altering idea that we are as God created us, perfect in His Sight. This is what God knows us to be, for as He is, so is His Son. We who dwell in an ego world do not believe this to be so and have been convinced by the deceitful ego mind that we are the home of evil, darkness and sin.

According to *A Course in Miracles*, we have mistakenly substituted this false perception of ourselves in the place of our True Nature. In actuality, what is unalterable is the Source of Life and Light that resides eternally within beyond time and space. It is with us wherever we go and in whatever we do. This is Truth, but it is hidden from our awareness by a dense cloud of denial that has shut out its Light. Why would we have done this to ourselves, even if it is subliminal? Answers to this question return us to the ontological story in the next section. Our resulting belief in the ego's precepts has affected every aspect of our world as we see it.

Let us now accept the idea of our indwelling Divinity that is with us always, and overcome the aberrant thoughts with which we have enshrouded ourselves. This is when we will burst out of the nightmare and behold all that is Real, and know ourselves as the One Son. The following excerpt from a Workbook lesson parallels these points.

'Deep within you is everything that is perfect, ready to radiate through you and out into the world. It will cure all sorrow and pain and fear and loss because it will heal the mind that thought these things were real, and suffered out of its allegiance to them.'[2]

The ego is comprised of an erroneous thought system that we have upheld and identified with, and has produced a false, limited self concept.

The *Course* further defines the ego as:

'...the sign of a limited and separated self, born in a body, doomed to suffer and to end its life in death...In fear it stands beyond the Everywhere, apart from All, in separation from the Infinite...'[3]

From this place of desolation we cry out in loneliness and despair. Our only hope lies with the Holy Spirit Who can lead us to our Reality and the knowledge of our Father's Love that has never wavered.

In the Workbook we are given hope of deliverance as it continues:

'To know reality is not to see the ego and its thoughts, its works, its acts, its laws and its beliefs, its dreams, its hopes, its plans for its salvation and the cost belief in it entails...(for) the Son of God is egoless. What can he know of fear and punishment, of sin and guilt, of hatred and attack, when all there is surrounding him is everlasting peace...in deepest silence and tranquility?'[4]

This is the Son as he truly is, not as we have fragmented and compartmentalized him to be.

As we further discuss the contrasts between the ego's wrong minded thought system and the Holy Spirit's right minded thought system, we will be using this understanding as our metaphysical definition of the ego.

As Jesus continually addresses the contrasts between these two thought systems, we become aware of their differences and are able to make a choice between those two opposed ways of thinking. It is important not to deny what our eyes see, but to interpret *what* they see differently. As we are guided by the Holy Spirit and are consistent in our endeavors, this distinctive mode of thinking does come about and our eyes will rest upon all people, events and circumstances with non-judgment and understanding.

We begin to understand that every interaction that transpires in this world is either Love or a call for Love, (in other words, we all are either exemplifying our Father's Love or are calling for His Peace and Understanding). So as our minds slowly change about transpiring events and interactions, it reflects how our inward thoughts are transforming and realigning with the Divine.

As we ask to see through the eyes of Truth and not of judgment, we are letting go of the ego's thought system and beginning to think with the Holy Spirit. Our goal is not to change our behavior but to change our thinking about the world, and then everything will fall into its proper place. As we move through these pages we will examine different strategies that will help us adopt these ideas as our own.

Chapter Four

Unfolding Insights

Before we go on, we will review the *Course's* foundational assessment on the creation of the world. This will give us a preliminary understanding of the subconscious motivating factors within ourselves, and we can gain an insight as to why we sometimes do things that we regret. As Saint Paul has said, 'For the good that I would I do not: but the evil which I would not, that I do.'[1]

To understand our subconscious motivations better, let us take another look at non-dualism. As we remember, non-dualism is comprised of the understanding that nothing exists but the all encompassing Oneness of God. If we can accept this to be the case, (at least intellectually) then logically there cannot be anything that Oneness is not. Shankara,[2] an ancient master of the non-dualistic Vedanta philosophy, defines Absolute Reality as that which never changes, and he considers only what is permanent to be 'real'.

These ideas open up a whole new avenue of thought, for if Reality is comprised of only that which is permanent, where does that leave us as transitory, impermanent individuals? Shankara relays that our one and only constant feature is the profound Reality of the Absolute Self, and our Absolute Self is One with God. When we reach this state of awareness, all thoughts of multiplicity cease and we recognize our Oneness with our Real Self.

At this point in our personal journey however, we are not in touch with that higher aspect of ourselves because we have superimposed individuality and separation upon the Undivided One and have thereby concealed our Real Self from our awareness. The world is then seen as divided and sub-divided, resulting in a multitude of seemingly disassociated fragments. This has led to the belief that we are individual identities living in a world of materialistic multiplicity.

As we mistakenly superimposed this idea of a personal self onto Absolute Existence, Shankara teaches that we thought that we could 'own' a piece of Existence and make it our own private property. Since we have identified with this belief, it results in our experience of a world. The world-appearance seems to be, but still, it is not. (See Appendix C)

This illusion of the world-phenomena will continue throughout our lives until we endeavor to find our true Reality. If we make a continuous effort to objectively 'step back' from our concrete thoughts about the world, our thoughts about its reality will begin to loosen their hold on our perceptions. The import that we have placed on the physical form will recede and we will behold the essence in Whose Image we are made. This vision of our Real Self will reveal our true Existence, for we have always existed, just not how we thought that we did.

As we now look at the world of duality, we must be fearless and admit that this world of differences is comprised of nothing more than characters acting upon a stage and playing to an illusory audience, for we have come to realize that only the Unchanging is permanent and everlasting.

This dream-like existence that we consider to be reality is reminiscent of the story of Plato's Cave[3], where prisoners are chained to their chairs and can only look forward toward a wall of shadows. A fire casts the silhouettes of real life images from behind them onto the wall, but they cannot turn to see the source of the light or the real activity. Because they see nothing else, the chained people do not know they are viewing only an apparition of life.

We are assisted with these ideas by having the contrasts between the Reality of our One Self and the illusory ego world of our own making revealed throughout the pages of *A Course in Miracles*. The *Course* is built upon these contrasts and is constructed from the understanding of the account of our beginnings. This understanding is fundamental to appreciating the reasons why we live in a world of individuality and differences, the rationale of our actions, and how we can surmount the obstacles with which we have ensnared ourselves.

This formation story is also depicted in Gary Renard's work as well as in much of the work by Dr. Kenneth Wapnick. Dr. Wapnick is a renowned clinical psychologist who is considered by many to be the foremost authority on *A Course in Miracles*. He was a friend to Helen Schucman and Bill Thetford, and has been involved in writing and teaching the *Course's* principles since 1973.

As we delve into the philosophy of *A Course in Miracles*, we come to the understanding that the Universe has always been in unity with God, but for the briefest of instances the Sonship had a 'tiny mad idea'[4] that wanted special attention from the Divine. God did not respond, since He cannot see apart from the Oneness of Himself, and the Son fell into the belief that he could separate from his Source and be autonomous. Even though he has always been a Thought in the Mind of God, he claimed that the independence from his Source was credible and real, and thus the desire for a dream of specialness became his reality.

The only *real* problem that we have, and that is depicted in countless ways, is that the Son did not realize that ideas cannot leave their Source. How can a thought be divided or torn asunder if the Son is a thought (idea) in God's Mind? The Son did not realize that he is forever One and that he could never separate from the Unity that is himself.

This is a central theme of *A Course in Miracles* and we are guided throughout its pages to come to this awareness for ourselves. The Son has merely forgotten that he could never be different from his Source and that even now he rests in his

Father's enfolding embrace. The dream of separation is only a *belief* that there was a disconnection from the Divine, as well as the mistaken belief that all else, including the Divine is outside of him. The Reality of the Son exists eternally in the Oneness that Is.

We will come back to this important point repeatedly, for taking the world seriously is a major obstacle that we must endeavor to train our mind to look beyond. To overcome this obstacle of duality is a process that requires a great deal of diligence because the subconscious resistance to embracing our Oneness is suppressed and out of our conscious awareness.

Now, returning to the story of our creation in form, the part of our mind that decided to be autonomous and separate (in theory) from our Source is referred to as the ego. Conversely, the Voice of the Holy Spirit always speaks within and quietly reminds us of our undivided, inherent Divinity. As we are reminded that there is a choice as to which belief system we want to embrace, we find that we are no longer imprisoned by our worldly constructs with no way out. We can choose to change our thinking about the nature of our reality, and leap back into the arms of Love from which we came and from which we in fact have never left. We will still operate in the world, but we will do so with a mindset that has Reality as its foundation.

One of the principles of the dream of division is that once a choice is made for a thought system, the previous thought system is forgotten. This forgetfulness finalized the deal, for not only was the ego thought system accepted as reality but the Holy Spirit's salvation has been promptly forgotten and sublimated. So in the dream of separation the Son has forgotten his true Identity of Oneness joined as One. Now that he thinks the destruction of God's Oneness was accomplished, he dreamed an even more frightful dream.

Because of his aforementioned 'amnesia' and the complete immersion in the ego's agenda, he now believes the ego's mad

29

story that God would allow lethal retribution for the 'treachery' that destroyed His Wholeness.

Thus, in self-defense, the Son's consciousness *appeared* to shift from the Oneness of Spirit and splinter into billions of separate fragments of form. Now we have the appearance of a physical world that is used as a projected screen of defense and stands between ourselves and our Father. As we have gotten lost in appearances, this projection of forgetfulness has been used to hide from the fearful thoughts of retribution when we 'disconnected' from our Source. It is this deeply sublimated fear that we are referring to anytime fear is mentioned.

These thoughts are so deeply buried that even though they are no longer confronted directly, they still leave us with a primeval sense of doom. It is here in this world of our own making that we have remained, with suffering and pain woven throughout our lives, and not understood why. We have not realized as yet that this whole set-up is a misperception, for our Father loves us unconditionally and completely.

As part of the whole dream scenario, we have compounded our lives by innumerable problems that have kept us perpetually occupied so that we would never look within to find the Holy Spirit's glad tidings that that our fears are unwarranted and that we are forever beloved. We have become solidly encased in a misleading thought construct that we are subconsciously motivated by but do not know how or why. Since we are so firmly ensconced in this thought system, the ego will never have its sovereignty questioned, and as we remain imprisoned within the ego's grasp we will never look above its narrow horizon toward the Light. Only with Divine Guidance can we starkly look at the contrasts of light and darkness in the world and rise above the dream to realize who we are outside of this illusion.

We will come to realize that even though this legend purportedly happened in the far distant past, this thought system that is comprised of the fear and guilt of the separation affects every aspect of our lives today; everything that we see, do, and feel, and every thought that we have. All that we perceive in the world is a symbolic representation of this original 'split'. We have used the chimera of form as a safety device to keep the world in place and God outside of us. This keeps our core fears at bay but it is at the cost of feeling alone and separate from our Source.

These may be new ideas that we are unfamiliar with, but as we begin to understand our subconscious motivations we will be able to decipher their significance in our lives. Truly, our only problem is the belief that the impermanent, ever-changing world is real and credible. Based on these principles of the *Course*, anything in existence other than Love is simply an illusion that is based on fear. Presently, for various reasons, we are still afraid to look upon the flawless Love that rests in our eternal Oneness, afraid of losing ourselves in the All. At this point it is important to seek the guidance of the Holy Spirit and Jesus so that we can find our way out of this self-inflicted thought construct.

We who have studied these and other texts throughout our lives have come to realize that we want to manifest our inherent God Reality. To do so, our task becomes to forgive the rest of the Sonship that fractured with us *and* ourselves for believing in the falsehood of separation, punishment and attack. As we choose to not listen to the ego's strident voice which has given us nothing that we have really wanted; it is then that we will hear our Father speak to us 'through His appointed Voice, which silences the thunder of the meaningless and shows the way to peace...'[5]

We are never separate from our Source, Who loves us as He loves Himself. We come to realize that our Father would never condemn or chastise us for errors in our thinking; for He does not see us as apart from Himself. *We* have made the mistake of believing that the errors were real. *We* are the ones who think we are separate. *We* are the ones who believe the error that we are disconnected from our Source, and we are the only ones who can heal this thought of division that we have put into play. Even though we have outwardly given credence to the ego's world, we can hear God's appointed Voice as He speaks to the Presence of the One Son within us. Even though the Holy Spirit is not part of the dream world, His helping hand reaches through the miasma and His radiant touch dispels all errors in thought.

Throughout these pages we have and will be elaborating and expanding upon these thoughts as we continually add a storehouse of new definitions to many of our previously held interpretations. We will also see some interesting parallels between these ideas and *The Gospel of Thomas*.

A notable observation about Thomas' gospel is, among other things that Jesus has repeatedly acknowledged the Oneness of God's Son, and he says that we all share in the unity of God's Creative Love. The truth of this unalterable principle has never changed despite our erroneous belief arising from the ego's depths that we are tainted and sinful. God is not vengeful, partisan, or angry. The Absolute Love of our Father is a perpetual fount that flows endlessly through our perceived errors and washes them away as if they never were.

To put these ideas into perspective, a question we can logically ask ourselves is why would a Father be angry with His Son who has made the mistake of holding onto a past that is not his true reality and has not happened? Errors can be and are easily corrected by a change of thought to a different Teacher, and the Father's Son can be liberated from the erroneous concepts that he had previously given credence to. As we begin to rely on and accept the loving thoughts and direction of the Holy Spirit, we will be led incrementally forward to embrace this 'new' way of thinking that reveals the ever-present splendor of our Unity.

This gift of knowledge that shows us how we can correct our thoughts to those of our Father is a miraculous gift given to us in love by the Holy Spirit. As we move forward in our thought processes and cast out our illusory concepts, we find that we are immersed in miracles and that 'Every miracle is but the end of an illusion.'[6]

We now hear the ring of Truth of these teachings with our inner ear and move forward to embrace this life changing thought system. Nevertheless, let us be aware that as we begin our journey, that we are in some regard striving for something that is beyond our ken and may at first have to accept its existence on faith.

...to ask for it implies the mind has been made ready to conceive of what it cannot see and does not understand. Yet faith will bring its witnesses to show that what it rested on is really there. And thus the miracle will justify your faith in it, and show it rested on a world more real than what you saw before; a world redeemed from what you thought was there.[7]

And thus our life's vision is truly changed and we see Reality for what it is. Our aspiration to choose a different way of thinking is a stepping stone to having an *experience* of God's Love. In that Holy Instant, we comprehend who we are, an indivisible part of the Whole. We realize that we may have made mistakes, but these errors do not stand in our way. As they fade away into insignificance, we realize that we are comprised of the Peace and Love that surpasses all understanding, and in that certain knowledge we assume our rightful place as God's One Son.

Chapter Five

The Perception of Sin

We have been immersed in the ego mindset that has believed that outside forces impinged upon us, and that we were prey to the ravages of our environment and subject to its fickle whims. We also have subconsciously believed ourselves to be eternal wrong-doers with no hope of redemption, and there is no escape from the unalterable mistakes that are called sins. Our belief is that the ultimate, unforgivable sin occurred when we fractured from the Divine, creating the 'separation'. This is the detrimental subconscious 'engine' that drives us and the world.

The ego fervently propagates a sense of unworthiness to keep us ever distant from our goal of finding our True Self. To keep its autonomy, it must keep the separation thought in place. If we look in the dictionary[1] we find that the definition of sin is the 'Transgression of divine law...any reprehensible action; serious fault or offense.'

The dictionary's version brings to mind the serious sins relayed in the Ten Commandments of the Bible, such as murder, adultery, covetousness...These definitions however, do not delve as deeply into the depths of the all-inclusive and pervasive nature of what we subconsciously perceive sin to be.

We can understand the workings of the ego better if we realize that it uses our sense of sin very subtly against us, and how it affects every aspect of our thoughts. The sins of the ego do not have to be gigantic in scope but are an intrinsic part of the subtle guilt that crops up in many, if not all of our interactions. Maybe we feel that we do not say or do the right thing, or we feel guilty because we have succumbed to malicious thoughts. Perhaps we feel a sense of unworthiness for not giving an acceptable amount of time, money or effort to a particular endeavor, or maybe it is a feeling of just not being good enough. Whatever it is, it is a no-win situation because the ego mind holds the yardstick that measures out what 'enough' is.

Thus the guilt emerges from the recesses of our minds and is translated into a perceived sin that subtly sneaks under our radar to make us feel inadequate. We feel guilty but don't why. What we have done is stepped over the edge of the abyss into the ego's jurisdiction of self-reproach. The buried, unconscious, unforgivable sin that we believe we have committed against our Father now rears its ugly head, and we are not even consciously aware of it.

We now see that it does not have to be a 'big' sin to send us into a tailspin of shame and remorse. The ego continually manipulates us by these subtle 'little' sins and will constantly replay them to keep us perpetually off balance.

An important point to be aware of is that any interactions with our brother and any thoughts about ourselves are a *reflection of our relationship with our Father*. So as we commit these minor (or major) sins against our brother we subconsciously translate them into sins against the Divine, hence our recurring guilty feelings. In fact, our whole world is a continuing saga that plays out this subconscious guilt repeatedly. We can see how our erroneous thoughts have crowded and darkened the screen of our vision and have blotted out the sight of our Father's Love. We look forward to the day that shall come, where we will transcend this worn-out script and step over the threshold into the real world of joy and peace.

As we now know, the self-recriminations for all major and minor sins come from our ego mind. The ego's sole purpose is to keep us embroiled in its world by whatever means, for that ensures its survival. Our objective is not to battle the ego (for that attention gives it legitimacy and credibility), but to recognize the unreality of its foundational thought of fear of reprisals and annihilation.

The *Course* is an excellent aid on our spiritual journey, for it brings to our attention that these two contrasting thought systems exist, and that we have the ability to make a choice between them. The more we recognize the ego for what it is, the more we will feel that we can safely let that thought process fade away. To free ourselves, we must realize that this burden of guilt that we have unwittingly agreed to take on is only a result of *our having confused sin with error.*

These sins that seemed to have happened as we listened to the wrong thought system, subtle or otherwise, are errors that happen in the world of form and cannot make God angry for they are not seen by Him and do not exist in His Mind. Logically, God as Pure Love and Light cannot hold even a particle of darkness within His Gaze, for then He wouldn't be a complete manifestation of Love.

The world of loss and suffering is fabricated in *our* ego mind and occurs in a self-contained separate dream of which He is not a part of nor has He made. God loves the 'Dreamer' unequivocally, even as He disregards the dream. There have been no offenses committed against Him, for the concept of sin is only an aspect the ego mind that has no conception of who the unified One Son is or Who our loving Father is. There is nothing that can change or compromise the Image in which we are made.

Since we have believed in the reality of the ego's world, we have been deceived into performing as the ego expected. As the examples of the following dramas unfold, let us keep in mind that even as we believed these false perceptions to be true, we have only made a mistake and have not done anything that cannot be undone by a shift in thought to a different Teacher. As we come to understand our mistaken concepts and are securely enfolded in the knowledge of our Father's Love we will we lightly laugh at the erroneous psychology of our self-imposed foibles.

We have been ruled subconsciously by our ego which has

always operated from a fearful foundation. This fear has bubbled up to the surface in countless ways to leave us with an appearance of many different problems. Since we did not realize that we had believed in a misperception of reality, we have tried to prove to ourselves and others that *we* have not committed any wrong doing.

To take the spotlight off of ourselves and to lift these sins from our shoulders, our only recourse was to cast them out onto our brother. This is the mainstay of the ego thought system, and is referred to throughout *A Course in Miracles* as 'projection'.

We have needed a person, object or circumstance to throw *our* guilt onto so that *they* would become the reflection of the guilt that we did not want to see in ourselves. We have projected that fearful belief of these 'unalterable' sins out onto others and proclaimed judgment upon them, even as we have turned away from that judgment in ourselves. The suffering images that we see are a vestige of the original projection (or dream), and we keep them in place to protect ourselves from the subconscious guilt that threatens to rise up out of the depths of our unconscious.

This means that we immediately project our guilt outward to be displayed on the screen of the world, so that the world now appears to victimize us. Now the world, which is an 'effect' of a thought, seems to become the 'cause' of our distress. This scenario is played out in numerous ways, where we feel 'victimized' in our jobs, by employers or employees, in family situations, by our parents, siblings, children, etc., etc. It is acted out in 'little' and 'big' altercations, but above all, acted out in situations that that we believe are happening *to* us, but that we are not responsible for.

As the blame was cast outward, we not only concealed the guilt from our awareness but have unwittingly kept ourselves separated from the Divine. We have identified with the concepts of this world (I am rich, poor, tall, short, thin, fat, sad, happy, depressed...) and believed that this is who we are. We have gathered up all of these fragmentary thoughts and built ourselves an image.

Let us take the view that these ideas are all misperceptions of who we really are, and those misperceptions can be considered to be a distinct separate energy force that is orbiting around our True Nature (much as the electrons of an atom orbit the nucleus). Because we are giving less and less credence to this dark energy cloud circling us, its hold on our consciousness will loosen and we will begin to merge with our Real Self. Our awareness will begin to turn away from giving import to the 'effects' of the dream, and we will tap into the Universal One Mind that transcends every effect. Constant awareness of our thoughts is the key to our salvation; this is what it means to be vigilant for the Kingdom.

To gain an understanding of how we have come to believe so wholeheartedly in this world of appearances, the following excerpt shows us how well we have been taught by the ego.

The learning of the world is built upon a concept of the self adjusted to the world's reality. It fits it well...The building of a concept of the self is what the learning of the world is for. This is its purpose that you come without a self, and make one as you go along. And by the time you reach 'maturity' you have perfected it... (This concept of yourself) bears no likeness to yourself at all... (but is) made to take the place of your reality as (a) Son of God.[2]

The *Course* asserts that we have an egoic concept of ourselves that has been developed over time. It is a completely false concept but we have embraced this fictitious self as real. We have fabricated a counterfeit identity that is presented to a world that believes in it and of which it is a part.

As we believed it real, we have had to continually prove to the world and to ourselves that our virtuous outward persona was genuine, but have secretly feared the exposure of its disingenuous base. We can see how we could have thought that this false identity was our self, and why we supported its authenticity and have continually justified its existence. We have been taught very thoroughly throughout our lives to overlook our Reality as a Son of God and have not as yet realized our mistaken choice.

The question we need to sincerely ask ourselves is; what if we firmly grasped the Holy Spirit's hand and bravely looked within? What do we think we would see? Our fear is that we would see desolation, but the truth is that we would see the Light of our Creation, the Love in Whose Image and likeness we are made. This is our True Image and it transcends all illusions.

With the gentle teachings from the *Course*, we will be guided to the awareness that we rest in God outside of time and space-even if we are not consciously aware of it. Even as this Truth is understood on inner levels, the *Course's* teachings strive to bring this awareness to the fore. We can now rely on the Holy Spirit Who knows the One Answer, and holds the key that will free us and give us rest in the Divine Embrace.

Our plea for Divine intervention is always heard, for Truth can be heard in the dream, even though it is not part of it. We hear the immediate response of our Redeemer that gently gives us an alternative, and as we listen our salvation is secured.

Chapter Six

A Discourse on Judgment

There are specific methods to re-establish the thought system of uncompromising Love and to remember our Father. One of the key thoughts to do so is to realize that we need to relinquish our personal judgments of our brother. Once we have recognized *why* we feel a need to condemn, criticize, or attack others, then we become aware that these judgments have not served us. In fact, those disparaging thoughts have resulted in leading us far away from the serenity that we have sought. Now we are beginning to understand the deep seated reasons for our fear and why we have this propensity to condemn and judge.

The world of form seems to be a very real nightmare of perceptions, judgments and sin. Since we have embraced it as real, our fearful belief in it has stifled the awareness of our true Reality and obscured the pure vision of who we really are, as One in Spirit.

Nevertheless, even though we may not outwardly experience it, we are still in the One mind that transcends all dimensions *now*. To experience this expanded awareness, we must make the choice to relinquish our own narrow views of the ego's judgment and conscientiously use the forgiveness principles.

The Workbook of the *Course* says: 'No one can judge on partial evidence. That is not judgment. It is merely an opinion based on ignorance and doubt. Its seeming certainty is but a cloak for the uncertainty it would conceal.'[1]

Here again, our inability to judge accurately is emphasized, for this partial evidence would be our narrow 'glimpse' into another's life, where it is obvious we could never have enough information to make an accurate assessment. We come to realize that as we judge the behaviors and actions of the world, which are in themselves illusory, our *one* problem still remains. That problem is the belief that we are separate from the Divine and then we conduct our lives as if this were so.

As we have discussed, the first step in overcoming this mindset is to understand that we have made a mistake by believing that this world is all that there is, and it has therefore become the gauge by which we have measured ourselves to be 'good' or 'bad'. We have put limitations upon ourselves that have blinded us to our Reality beyond form. This does not mean that we ignore the world and keep our heads in the clouds, but it does mean that we need to change our perspectives. We can keep in mind that anything that changes, alters or perishes is part of the ego mindset and is not of the eternal Oneness that Is.

Let us come to rely on the Holy Spirit's judgment, for even as He knows the cause of our underlying *one* problem which has multiplied into all of our self-made complexities, He is with us eternally and stands for our memory of God. He sees all time in its entirety, both backwards and forward. As He knows the end from the beginning, we can trust that He will lead us forward safely. The Holy Spirit is a Divine Mediator between the two worlds, He knows the Truth and knows the remedy.

(The Holy Spirit) ...will not tell you that your brother should be judged by what your eyes behold in him, nor what his body's mouth says to your ears...He passes by such idle witnesses, which merely bear false witness to God's Son...He recognizes only what God Loves, (and) all the ego's dreams of what you are vanish before the splendor He beholds.[2]

Jesus, in the Text of the *Course* beckons us to rely on the Holy Spirit, for He perceives the *cause*;

How else could He correct your error, (you) who have

overlooked the cause entirely? He bids you bring each terrible effect to Him that you may look together on its foolish cause...*You* judge effects, but *He* has judged their cause. And by His judgments are effects removed.[3]

These passages amplify our understanding of the premise of cause and effect. The palpable forms that we perceive are a physical consequence of an inaccurate *thought*, and it is that erroneous thought that is the underlying cause of all that we see.

We (as the Universal One Son) are the creator of what we want to see in the world of form. These images are brought to the forefront of our minds to 'see' a world that we wish to behold. Who we really are, the One Son, actually dwells outside of time and space and but chooses to 'look in' and see certain images out-pictured in the world. We are looking through the eyes of those images and believe that we experience all of the events that taking place. We completely accept what we see in the world as reality, but are actually turning away from true vision that would show us unequivocal Love that is everlasting. We have an unwarranted fear of rejection and a sense of unworthiness that keeps these separation ideas in place. Let us remember that all of these thoughts and motivations are taking place beyond our waking awareness. Our objective is to methodically unearth all of the subconscious debris that is obscuring our true vision. These are challenging metaphysical concepts to embrace, for they run contrary to all that we currently uphold as real.

There is an interesting source of information from the scientific community that runs parallel to these metaphysical ideas, and gives us pause as to our unquestioned ideas about what we have always considered to be a solid reality. In his book, *The Holographic Universe*, Michael Talbot relays that there is growing evidence, especially among quantum physicists, that 'the universe itself is a kind of giant hologram, a splendidly detailed illusion...there is evidence to suggest that our world and everything in it – from snowflakes to maple trees to falling stars and spinning electrons – are also only ghostly images, projections from a level of reality so beyond our own it is literally beyond both space and time.'[4] Talbot goes on to detail scientific studies that explain and support these remarkable findings.

So as perception follows judgment, our wish for an effect in the world to be real does not make that image reality. If we want true vision, and desire to see the real world versus the broken world of our own making, we can give our judgments and interpretations over to the Holy Spirit and consistently ask for His intercession to see things differently. As we call upon Him, we have the confidence that the He knows the cause and sees the effect, and will thereby make an accurate judgment for God's Will on our behalf. We are comforted by the knowledge that the perfect outcome of loving forgiveness will prevail, for the Holy Spirit knows that God's Eternal Son has only dreamt the nightmare of vengeance and attack.

An exercise in mind control that will help us look within and calm our inner conflicts is outlined in the Text;

Let us be still an instant, and forget all things we ever learned, all thoughts we had, and every preconception that we hold of what things mean and what their purpose is. Let us remember not our own ideas of what the world is for. We do not know. Let every image held of everyone be loosened from our minds and swept away. Be innocent of judgment, unaware of any thoughts of evil or of good that ever crossed your mind of anyone. Now do you know him not. But you are free to learn of him, and learn of him anew, without the past that sentenced him to die, and you with him. Now is he free to live as you are free, because an ancient learning passed away, and left a place for truth to be reborn.[5]

To review and summarize these ideas then, our first step in

seeing our brother in a new light is for us to overlook and set aside our past judgments of him. We recognize that we have misjudged him from our own limited perspectives, and at this time we are willing to give those short-sighted judgments over to the Holy Spirit to rectify. As we use the above exercise from the Text, we trust that He will judge truly and will give the One Answer that will relieve us of a sense of burden and make clear the means of our salvation.

Judgment as Interpretation
Let us be aware that as we interact with others we are not responding to anything directly but indirectly. This means that we respond to our *interpretation* of a particular action or event based on our past experiences and not on what seems to be currently happening at all. We may have thought that we were making practical judgments and actions, but we have only been seeing through a distorted lens that had given us a warped illusion of reality. Our true clarity of thought has been obscured by past judgments that have waited in the shadows to ambush us.

As we examine the word 'interpretation', we are reminded of the old adage about looking at a glass of water as either half empty or half full. Both interpretations are accurate, but it is our personal past experiences that gives rise to *our* interpretation of it as either half empty or full.

We can understand the concept of interpretation better if we admit that our brother can see the contents of the glass either way, but even if his observations are different we realize that those observations are no less valid than our own. To judge against him for a different interpretation would be foolhardy.

If we generalize this idea, we recognize that we cannot judge anything in this world as being the absolute truth since our judgments are based on our own past experiences and impressions. We have even seen how many times our preconceived notions have been inaccurate. The events in question are only our point of view where *we* have judged or labeled them to be either 'half-empty' or 'half-full'.

Further, as we take the precepts of the *Course* to heart, let us recognize that all we are really doing is judging between two illusions in the egoic world, both of which have nothing to do with the thought system of our salvation. Ultimately, to make judgments in this world of opposites, or become embroiled in debates over various points of view is a misuse of time, and serves as a delay tactic in coming to terms with who we are in Truth beyond time and space.

We have further sustained the ego thought system and thereby our world by subconsciously *wanting* our brother to have a different interpretation of events. We orchestrate disputes that justify our judgment of his positive or negative interpretations in order to make ourselves 'right' and him 'wrong'.

The bottom line is that we raise a projected image to stand between ourselves and our Father to offset and protect ourselves from His Gaze. As we recognize the absurdity of these subconscious thoughts of retribution and vengeance, the defenses that we have made up will be slowly dismantled and we will see the Truth.

Again, even though we may have forgotten our connection to the Divine and have blindly stumbled along leaving judgmental errors in our wake, all that is needed to correct these mistakes is to exchange our previous teacher for the One Who has always been our Advocate. We have the comforting reassurance that there is nothing that we could do in the world that could possibly sever or destroy the relationship we have with our Father, Who always has loved us truly and forever. So now more than ever, we need the help of the Holy Spirit, Who will help bring us around to right-minded thinking. When any negative momentum arises, we now have the advantage of using our new found ability to choose differently.

Our thoughts will change for the better when we decide to

accept the Atonement for ourselves. Then we will finally be able to accept our Father's unequivocal Love into our lives and no longer kick against the thorns in an attempt to punish ourselves for what we have not done.

The *Course's* definition of the Atonement principle reveals that we do not have separate interests from each other but have one common goal of reuniting with our Father. In the Atonement there is no sacrifice in thought, word or deed. It is simply a correction (or undoing) of the one mistake that the Son made, where he gave the error a reality it did not have and kept the 'separation' thought in place.

As the One Son, our one and only interest is to reunite our thoughts together again. To do so, we begin by allowing ourselves to be guided on the path that corrects the errors of our thinking. We will be brought gently to the awareness of our unity that will help us to gently overcome the fearful thought of separation.

Forgiveness that sees all events and circumstances as love or a call for love is a key concept in helping us to be able to do so. Any attack, verbal or otherwise, subconsciously reflects the Son's silent appeal for the understanding and love of his Father. As we are ultimately One with our brother as our One Self, we answer *our own* call for love and understanding when we respond to any situation with love and not condemnation, for we also have felt deprived of our Father's Love. We, as well as our brother, have desperately sought to be forgiven for those things that we thought we have done, and our silent plea has always been to know that we have not trampled on our Father's Love. In an effort of self-preservation we had projected that unwanted sense of guilt out onto our brother. But now, in light of our new under-standing we will release these faulty judgments into the Holy Spirit's hands and will find that those projected attack thoughts will gently dwindle away leaving only happiness in their place.

To pull together all of the preceding ideas then, each and

every encounter that happens in our lives is neutral in and of itself. *We* are the ones who subconsciously assign to impartial events an interpretation that gives them an emotional charge. If we see a world of suffering and loss, it reveals how we are paying homage to the egos interpretations, versus seeing the Essential Spirit beyond form. We have only made the mistake of choosing the wrong teacher to paint upon our neutral canvas. We have not allowed the Truth to shine away the confusion that would reveal what is holy, pure and true about ourselves. It is here that we need to call for the assistance of the Holy Spirit; for He is the only One Who can lead us out of the confusion of our misperceptions.

As we come to understand that we are not different or separate from our brother or the One that is, we can then choose to interpret our brother's attack, verbal or otherwise, as his call for love. We can also compassionately understand any 'closed-mindedness' in our brother for what it is. It is his fear of upsetting his presumably stable present with an alternative and therefore uncertain future. Consequently anyone who questions the perceived stability of his thoughts would inevitably be attacked by him either verbally or physically. These points are important to be aware of, for the more we understand our brother's motivations and projections, the more we understand our own.

As we are able to identify those negative thoughts and recognize their unreality, we are able to forgive them in both our brother and ourselves and then let them go. When we come to realize that these long held concepts have no power over us, *then* it does not matter how cruel our brother is, because we no longer identify with that aspect of the projection. Since the anger that we see in our brother is no longer part of ourselves, it cannot irritate, annoy us or disturb our peace anymore. We do not deny what our eyes behold, for it is still physically seen, but our interpretation of the form has changed. We are free of it because we realize that it is no longer a lingering aspect of ourselves to be gotten rid of; and we no longer have the need to project our guilt outward because the Light has shined it away.

If we want to see with the Holy Spirit's Vision, all we need to do is be aware of the ego's antics. The unbounded freedom to see with the candid sight of the Holy Spirit is one of the many wonderful gifts unveiled in *A Course in Miracles*.

We can now boldly look within and see that we are not the ego's home of evil, darkness or sin, but are as God created us, pure and holy in His Sight. There is nothing that we *or* our brother could have done (because any errors have only happened in a dream of transgressions) that could affect or alter our Father's Love for us. Once we recognize who we are beyond form, and see the ego's thought system for what it is, the flood-lights of recognition expose the darkness that we no longer want to identify with.

All is Not as it Appears
An interesting comment early in the Workbook relates to these points that we have been discussing. It speaks of thoughts as images that we have made, and because these thoughts appear as images in our minds we think them real, and do not recognize them as a fictitious invention.

There are some relevant parables that we will review shortly that follow along these lines, but for now we will take a look at a passage from the Workbook that also addresses these images;

...It is because the thoughts you think you think appear as images that you do not recognize them as nothing. You think you think them, and so you think you see them. This is how your 'seeing' was made. This is the function you have given your body's eyes. It is not seeing. It is image making. It takes the place of seeing, replacing vision with illusions.[6]

If we accept that the ego thoughts of this world produce meaningless images, we will gain further insights into the ego thought system and how it affects our perceptions. Now that we know that everything that we observe is an event that we have placed an interpretation upon, we see that we are accountable for how we think, and therefore responsible for our view of the world. Our choice of thought systems has affected our interpretation of what our senses see, hear, feel and touch. Since we have chosen the ego's world of judgment and division we can deduce from the above excerpt, that we have chosen the world of illusory image making.

There is only One Self that is connected beyond form to all of the lost fragments that have always been One. Now as we assist the figures and images in this world, what we are doing is healing our own thoughts and enfolding ourselves back into Divine Oneness.

As our beliefs and views about our brother change, we realize that he has done nothing but scrabble around in a dream from which he has not awoken. We understand this now because the Holy Spirit has guided us through the same nightmare. With His help we have overcome that self-same guilt that had projected identical thoughts of fear and blame. With new eyes we have confronted and dismissed the unreality of the fearful dream, and no longer fear to look within and see the shining radiance that was always there. We now have the ears to hear our brother's unspoken call for the same surcease from pain that we have had in the past. We can hear and respond to his call for the liberating Love that unbeknownst to him, has been forever his.

We have been given the joyful opportunity to share this happy news! Nothing even needs to be said, for as our brother recognizes the Truth that is shining within us, he knows, inwardly if not outwardly, that the Love of the Father belongs to him as well.

With renewed understanding, our forgiving hands offer the

comforting solace that flows through us and extends the Love of our Father to all of His Creation. This joyful extension of Love that we received of our Father is given to our brother through us, and then returned back to us through him, to only flow out again...

When we change our mind and accept our true Guide, the paradigm changes and then it is inevitable that our observations and judgments will take on a different interpretation. Obviously, we are still interacting in the world, but the difference is that we are 'not of it', and we are not caught up in its emotionally charged dramas. As we consistently choose God's Appointed Voice as our Escort, our mind is transformed and we will dwell in the real world that holds only peace.

Note that as we move forward on our personal journey, it is inevitable that we will alternate between the two teachers. However, with constancy and consistency we will find that we are abiding more and more with our Divine Guide and we will steadily come to discover that this is all there is.

Transcending our Judgments
Instead of focusing on the false perception of the ego and believing in its reality as we had in the past, let us endeavor to embrace the Holy Spirit's thoughts and His purpose as our own, inviting Love and forgiveness to replace the worrisome sights that we have made. We will then find that all judgments and criticisms fall away and we will finally look upon the sparkling world of our salvation. In the Text Jesus asks us metaphorically which thought system we desire to manifest;

> Would you not rather greet the summer sun than fix your gaze upon a disappearing snowflake, and shiver in remembrance of the winter's cold?[7]

The end result of our thoughts of judgment is to recognize that we have used them as a device to defend our illusions and misperceptions, and that we have employed them as a means to convince ourselves of the reality of the dream.

How does one overcome illusions? Surely not by force or anger, nor by opposing them in any way, merely by letting reason tell you that they contradict reality. They go against what must be true...What merely is needs no defense... (for) Love rests in certainty. Only uncertainty can be defensive. And all uncertainty is doubt about yourself.[8]

If we recognize that there is only one loving, all inclusive and simple response to every event and circumstance, we would compassionately identify any attack as only our brother's plea for help and not as a personal attack. It is then that our outlook is unwavering and that there is nothing that can disturb or shake our inner peace.

As we begin to trust in the Holy Spirit's judgment, we willingly give our personal judgments over to Him so that He can judge them unerringly. Now that we have commended our spirit to Him and His righteousness, we will find that this faithful trust was a 'prerequisite for hearing God's Voice,'[9] and now we shall hear.

Let us now ask the Holy Spirit for the experience to consciously hear God's Guiding Voice, and to have the continuous awareness of Him in the forefront of our mind. This is our inherent objective and our heart's desire.

Chapter Seven

The Dream

We will look at the dream of this world more thoroughly to better understand our split nature and how we can transcend it. As we go on, we will also see how *The Gospel of Thomas* parallels these ideas, and how Jesus has relayed a different message than we may at first have thought.

An important point to consider is that the reason we / others are innocent has nothing to do with the level of form. 'We are all equally innocent because *what we are seeing is not true*. This is *our* dream.'[1] Our eternal innocence is a representation of our Oneness in Spirit that never varies and is eternally constant, even though it is out of our awareness. We have only forgotten this Truth as we became caught up in the illusion of form.

These are the two worlds, or systems of thought that cannot overlap. Let us recall our ontological story where every rung of the ladder that was descended, the previous rung was forgotten. As this occurred, we also forgot our Source as we made our downward descent into the dream.

It cannot be over emphasized that as we speak of forgiveness, it is to have forgiving *thoughts* (not behaviors) in response to all of our interactions. When those forgiving thoughts are in place and we find that we need to physically do something thereafter, we do it. It is our *interpretation of the actions* that happen that is understood with the Holy Spirit's thought system. We need but to change our thinking back to our right mind. Let us have the courage to test the waters to see that this is so. We will find that we will not be mauled by fiendish creatures, but shall discover the Living Water of everlasting joy is waiting to fill our souls.

Since we are living in the world of our own creation, we need to deal with our physical surroundings in a responsible and pragmatic way. What becomes important is *how* and *what* we think as we deal with problems in the world so that we can free ourselves from the shackles that we have forged from our wrong minded thinking. We can see how our past judgmental thoughts have become a detour to our coming into alignment with Spirit, and we are now in the process of resetting our internal compass to chart a different course.

The teachings of Jesus in *A Course in Miracles* endeavors to open our minds to other possibilities that we may not have considered before. If one thinks about the dream state, we can all agree that we see moving pictures and images that may or may not normally be seen in our waking state, but nevertheless feel and look very real and evoke very real emotions. Let us now pause to consider what we are seeing with. Our eyes are closed and we may be lying in a bed, but we see ourselves in a park or office building. We would then have to admit we must be seeing with our minds.

'The truth is that when you are apparently awake during the day and you have your eyes open, it's not really the body's eyes you are seeing with any more than when you're asleep at night. It's *always* your mind that is seeing. It's *always* your mind that is hearing and feeling and doing the other things you give the body's senses credit for. There is no exception to this.'[2] It is as if there is a giant movie projector unreeling dreams in the theater of our mind. The *Course* supports this premise by saying:

> It seems the world determines what you perceive... (In actuality it is) your thoughts that determine the world you see...in this idea is your release made sure.[3]

The reuniting of the fragments of the splintered aspects of the Son of God is accomplished by a mind whose thoughts have merged with the Oneness that Is. This is the mind that Jesus had and what we are striving to get in touch with. We will find that as we accept our innocence, the guilt will fall away and the Light that we are and that has been obscured will shine once more in our awareness.

It is evident that it is only the thoughts in our minds that can join and that bodies cannot merge into Oneness. But we live with the perception that we are bodies and maintain a little 'fence' (the thought that we are separate) between ourselves and our brother. We keep up the illusion that we are separate and different instead of allowing the *thought* of our Unity to come to the fore to see beyond appearances. The belief in separated individuals in this world reflects the distressing thought that we are apart from all creation.

This idea of separation is a component of the 'great projection.'[4] As we remember, obstacles are projections that we have made real and have stumbled over on the road to Peace by not accepting our own worthiness of God's unconditional Love. By not accepting His Love as our just due, we remain alone and separate. If we judge our brother harshly (thus making him different from us), we keep these obstacles in place and are thereby inadvertently keeping ourselves separate from our Father as well.

Throughout the *Course,* Jesus assists us in overcoming these errors in our thinking by providing us with numerous Workbook lessons to contemplate. He repeatedly gives us examples of the contrasts between the Love that is our Everything, and the fear that is a product of the illusion. An excerpt from the *Course's* Text states:

> If you but recognized how little stands between you and your awareness of your union with your brother! Be not deceived by the illusions (presented) of size and thickness, weight, solidity and firmness of foundation. Yes, to the body's eyes it looks... immovable as is a mountain. Yet within you is a Force that no illusions can resist.[5]

That Force is the Truth of our Reality, and it is only the '...unwillingness to overlook what seems to stand between you and your brother that makes it look impenetrable, and defends the illusion of its immovability.'[6]

Once again, we are told that we are not only responsible for what we see, but accountable for what is manifest in our lives. If we strive to see beyond this opaque curtain that colors everything darkly, we will then behold Reality. An additional correlation to the above quote is the following Saying from *The Gospel of Thomas*.

Saying 48:
'If two make peace with each other in a single house, they will say to the mountain, 'Move over here!' and it will move.'

If we bring the illusions to the Truth, and consistently work to dissolve the ego thought system, then all that will be left is the Holy Spirit's right minded perspective containing the real world of peace and forgiveness. Our 'house' (mind) is then unified, our consciousness is single and our vision becomes clear. As our consciousness is unified it has the power, strength and love of the Creative Source to bring all circumstances into alignment with the Will of God. We now find that obstacles that are seemingly as big as a mountain diminish in their enormity.

Illusions are illusions and are false. Your preference gives them no reality. Not one is true in any way and all must yield with equal ease to what God gave as answer to them all. God's Will is One.[7]

These statements speak volumes, and if we can step out of the limiting parameters that we have set about ourselves, and truly consider the implications of these thoughts of liberation from the bonds of darkness and superstition, our freedom and release are only a small step away. We can see that what we had thought has its exact opposite in Truth. If we are open to the premise that all is not as we had thought it to be, and that our past decisions may not have been in our best interest, then we will begin to move forward and remove those mental obstacles that have precluded us from unifying our perceptions.

Some of the key concepts that our source books are trying to convey is a different perspective on what we consider reality. The ego would like us to focus only on the body and the world as our reality. Our true Reality, as cited in an earlier quote, is pure Mind, and we can come back to it by choosing to let the precepts of the Holy Spirit flow through us. These concepts will actually relieve our sense of struggle and strife as we realize we need do nothing[8] but let go of our active interference and accept our salvation. This means that there is no behavior or ritual that needs to be accomplished for there is nothing from without that can alter the Light from which we were created.

There is nothing that we need do or prepare for to make ourselves worthy of salvation, but indeed we do need, even if for an instant, to stop all *doing*, 'both physical and mental, and try to enter the moment of stillness where past, future and the body are forgotten.'[8A] Thus our vision of the world is healed and we are reconciled once again with our Source. It is important to remember that when we speak of the Holiness of the One Son, we are speaking of the unified Sonship as a thought in the Mind of God, and not of the individual bodies of mankind.

Our aim then, is to view everything with the eyes of the Holy Spirit, discerning between our valuable eternal treasure and that which is valueless[9], the empty offerings of the ego. As our discernment develops, we will move forward and come into alignment with our Father's Will, which is *our* will and our freedom from all illusions. Our 'house' where the Peace of God has always abided will once more be unified into its natural state, and we will be conflicted no more.

Chapter Eight

Forgiveness

One of the key components for us to return to our non-dualistic state of awareness that is emphasized both in the *Course* and the Sayings of Thomas is the process of advanced forgiveness. We have come to realize that the dream that we did not know we were in has obscured our memory of God. To re-establish the memory of our Divine estate, we are attempting to see beyond the dream and change the beliefs that we had about our brother. We have come to the realization that our view of him directly reflects our perception of ourselves and our world. As we strive to come up higher, our objective becomes to forgive him his errors, for we have recognized that only then can we forgive ourselves.

> Forgiveness recognizes what you thought your brother did to you has not occurred. It does not pardon sins and make them real. It sees there was no sin. And in that view are all your sins forgiven....An unforgiving thought is one which makes a judgment that it will not raise to doubt, although it is not true.[1]

This passage directs us to look within without fear with Jesus and see our sinlessness.

As the preface from the *Course* states;

> ...in this world, forgiveness is a necessary correction for all the mistakes that we have made. To offer forgiveness is the only way for us to have it, for it reflects the law of Heaven that giving and receiving are the same. Through forgiveness the

thinking of the world is reversed....by its mercy we can at last forgive ourselves. Holding no one prisoner to guilt, we become free. Acknowledging Christ in all our brothers, we recognize His Presence in ourselves.[2]

To further expand on this point and delineate the obstacles that stand in the way of our forward progression;

Let me not think that I can find the way to God, if I have hatred in my heart (unforgiveness). Let me not try to hurt God's Son, (in thought, word or deed) and think that I can know his Father or my Self.[3]

As a follow up to these thoughts, the Lesson Heading reaffirms the idea; 'To love my Father is to love His Son.'

The Workbook has many lessons that help us to focus on our right mind, and to realign our thinking to the Will of God. We come to realize that His Will is our will, and forgiveness is the means to trigger an experience to remember Him.

The greatest gift that we can give to our Father is to love our brother and forgive his seeming errors, and we do this by understanding that (1) those errors are not real (because they have occurred in a dream that our Father has no part of) and therefore (2) they haven't really happened, and that (3) we as the One Son are not different from each other or our Father, but are the same.

Then the miraculous happens, our True Nature beyond form shines forth through the form and the love that we are and the love that we have for our Father radiates out and is reflected back to Him. At that time the loving forgiveness that has been multiplied and expanded comes around full circle and we find that we have healed ourselves. It is here that we understand that giving and receiving are one and the same.

This idea is reminiscent of a passage in the New Testament where Jesus tells us to 'love our God with all our heart and soul, mind and strength, and love our neighbor as ourselves.'[4] There is no commandment greater than this. This ardor for our brother, ourselves, and God brings to the fore the love of the All which is One. The process of removing the barriers to Love that we have erected will heal the schism that we have put in place between ourselves and our God awareness.

There is a three step process that we can follow to activate the awareness of advanced forgiveness in our minds. The first component of this program of forgiveness is to concede that we are in a dream or illusion, even though we seem to perceive separate lives, with separate identities and all of their attendant problems. Our forms may be different, but the Spirit of God's Love dwells within us all. The One Son has compartmentalized himself and cut himself off from his true Identity to protect himself from an unwarranted fear of his own making.

If we realize that we are One in Reality, then logically, Wholeness cannot attack Itself or see Itself other than Whole, for that would be an impossibility in perfect Oneness. If this is so, then all that changes or is corruptible is by its very nature at variance with Wholeness and cannot bring lasting peace. As the *Course* relays;

As God created you, you must remain unchangeable, with transitory states by definition false. And that includes all shifts in feeling, alterations in conditions of the body and the mind; in all awareness and in all response.[5]

With this in mind, as we journey along life's highways and byways, we will come to the crossroad where we will determine, with divine help and vision, to surrender our thoughts of malice and judgment and choose the way of the Holy Spirit's path of Atonement. (The *Course's* definition of the Atonement is a correction of our thinking, or the undoing of the errors in our thoughts. There is no need to give up anything to 'atone' for perceived sins, because now we have accepted ourselves as God created us.) We find, to our heart's profound jubilation, the Holy Place of God is revealed to us from within, the real world rises to greet our sight, and we now know that the everlasting remembrance of God is not far behind. *A Course in Miracles* has a lovely vision:

All this beauty will rise to bless your sight as you look upon the world with forgiving eyes. For forgiveness literally transforms vision, and lets you see the real world reaching quietly and gently across chaos, removing all illusions that had twisted your perception and fixed it on the past.[6]

The above statement relays that the real world will be seen when we have given up the guilt and judgment that has tied us to the past and our dreams. We will see everything through forgiving eyes in the eternal present.

The real world cannot be perceived except through eyes forgiveness blesses...And the sights are gentle. Only happy sights and sounds can reach the mind that has forgiven itself...The world it sees arises from a mind at peace within itself.[7]

This excerpt discloses that it is possible to see this chaotic world with a sense of peace, for even as our forgiven minds acknowledge the outer physical conditions, it does not affect our inner state of serenity.

The second component in the process of forgiveness is forgiving both our projected images and ourselves for having the dream. As we ponder the thought of our Reality as Spirit and the fundamental unreality of form, we can then move on to forgive ourselves and take responsibility for dreaming up the whole debacle in the first place. As we think about the unreality of form (and our unity beyond it), we can look to change our mind so that we do not place such importance on physical events or disputes that occur, and we can strive to have the eternal essence of which we are comprised in the forefront of our mind.

We have touched upon this aspect of the 'making of the dream' previously. Suffice it to say, when we manifest forgiveness of all life, the purpose of the barriers we had set up between ourselves and God are dismantled. We will become connected to the peace of God that has always resided within.

This process of forgiveness of ourselves and our brothers is such that, 'The only way we can forgive what is within is to forgive what *seems* to be without. Until we learn how to forgive everything we see around us we will never be able to find our way out and escape the illusion and experience our own innocence and Divinity.'[8]

Our brother reflects back to us our own unconscious doubts and fears. As we look past the errors our brother has made and see the light beyond his physical form, we in turn realize we are forgiven for those self-same errors. It is enlightened self interest then, to look past the errors and form to forgive what has not happened. Remember, we are forgiving him for what he hasn't done and therefore by extension we are forgiving ourselves for what we haven't done, which was the thought that we had separated from God's Love. As we recognize and accept who our brother is, we then recognize our true Self and steadfastly come to the understanding that we are Whole. As we rise in consciousness above our previous precepts, we step outside of the dream and find that we all rest in the peace of God.[9]

This insightful awareness is indicated in the *Course* where Jesus says; 'You share no evil dreams if you forgive the dreamer, and perceive that he is not the dream he made.'[10] We are the Dreamer of the dream and as we forgive ourselves and our brother all illusions, we will come full circle and recognize that '...where you join His Son the Father is.'[11] Thus, the union of our minds proclaims our freedom from limitation and our return to our Father. This concept is also exemplified in the following Saying, where we seek to look beyond form.

Saying 75:
J said, 'There are many standing at the door, but those who are alone will enter the bridal suite.'

There are many who declare they want peace but still fight amongst themselves, claiming one thing and doing another, and are totally immersed in the world's concepts of reality. Their voices and hearts are not in accord, and chaos reigns. Our goal is to bring our thoughts into alignment with the Holy Spirit's precepts, unifying our thoughts by keeping our one purpose and who we are in the forefront of our minds. We can only enter the bridal suite with our brother unified in thought as our One Self. We accomplish this by seeing past the body to the indwelling Spirit, forgiving our brother for what he has not done and seeing him as he is, not as we have judged him to be. As we do so, the dross falls away, and we find our consciousness is once again united and we stand merged as God's One Son, purified to enter the bridal suite.

The third component of this three step program is to ask for help of the Holy Spirit and Jesus to guide us to see differently and to choose His strength.[12] To accomplish this task of regaining our unity, embracing forgiveness and reclaiming our Source, we need the guidance of the Holy Spirit to have the vision and strength to give up our judgments of our brother. We need His guidance for we have enmeshed ourselves too deeply in the veils of forget-fulness to do it alone, and where we still perceive our personal judgments to be 'right'. We must ask for and rely on His guidance until His vision becomes our own. He is the lamp that dispels the darkness and guides our way through the maze of shadows. Without His radiance to light our way, we would be lost in the world of form.

We have examined several words that had different meanings than we had previously assigned to them. We will look at another definition for the word 'resurrection'. The resurrection, in Christian terms, refers to the bodily resurrection of the righteous at the time of the Last Judgment. The *Course's* definition of the resurrection has nothing to do with the body or with a point in time, but is defined as the awakening of the mind to see the Truth of ourselves as Spirit, it is the 'undoing' of the separation thought. As we 'undo' these errors in our thinking, all that will be left is the shining radiance that we always were but had been obscured.

It is stated in *A Course in Miracles* that 'Your resurrection is your reawakening', [13] emphasizing that this is a study of the mind and not of bodily functions or behaviors. The resurrection of the Mind of God is as a phoenix rising out of the ashes of our preconceived precepts. All of the debris and malevolence falls away leaving only the magnificence of God shining in all of His splendor. Conversely, if we close our eyes to the Truth and hold grievances, we forget who we are and stay in the illusion. And who are we? In Truth, we are the Son of God, birthless, deathless, and changeless, joyfully abiding in the Oneness of our Father's Love forever.

The Workbook gives a beautiful description of the eternal majesty of God's Son, and is one among many that we can use as a meditative affirmation of our Divine Reality. It is a reflection of who we really are beyond time and space;

I am God's Son, complete and healed and whole, shining in the reflection of His Love. In me is His exceptional creation sanctified and guaranteed eternal life. In me is love perfected, fear impossible, and joy established without opposite. I am the holy home of God Himself. I am the Heaven where His Love resides. I am His holy Sinlessness Itself, for in my purity abides His Own.[14]

Since we have been mired in form identification, these thoughts on forgiveness, judgment and non-dualism will take time to absorb, as they run counter to our previously held ideas. It is difficult to change our minds as to who we and our brother are, *now*. All we need though, is a little willingness to begin. As the *Course's* Text says;

> This is the truth. At first to be but said and then repeated many times; and next to be accepted as but partly true, with many reservations. Then to be considered seriously more and more, and finally accepted as the truth.[15]

We have a choice as to which world we want to see, and once we have made that choice, we maintain it and uphold it continuously. Let us elect to put aside our previous choices that have obscured our True Reality and strive to embrace the Holy Spirit's ideas that will lead us to the real world.

> Choose, then, his body or his holiness as what you want to see, and which you choose is yours to look upon. Yet will you choose in countless situations, and through time that seems to have no end, until the truth be your decision (in every case). For eternity is not regained by still one more denial of Christ in him....The Christ in you beholds his holiness. Your specialness (ego) looks on his body and beholds him not.[16]

We choose and choose again, sometimes withdrawing from our quest, or possibly choosing wrongly, but our aim is certain in its ultimate victory, for it is God's Will. We may need to forgive ourselves as well, if only for our impatience that our goals are not manifesting immediately.

There is nothing 'unworthy' about us that prohibits the

manifestation of Spirit. What slows down the manifestation of our goals is a lifetime of fearful momentums and errors in our thinking that need to be undone in their own time sequence. This is why this lifelong curriculum requires such diligence and focus, so that we can slowly restructure our thinking and gradually realize that we live beyond the error. Jesus and the Holy Spirit are gently guiding us at our own pace and in divine order; so that when we are ready we can welcome eternal joy without fear or a sense of sacrifice.

Chapter Nine

The Double Shield

We are taught in *A Course in Miracles* and much of Dr. Wapnick's work that we are dreaming two dreams, or more specifically, a simultaneously occurring dream within a dream. The first 'secret' dream 'happens' in our ontological beginnings when we take the 'tiny mad idea' (a dream of separation) seriously. This then leads to the explosive second dream (or the 'world's dream' of form) that keeps that separation thought in place, evidenced by separated forms and bodies. This is where the One Son continues to dwell in illusions of his own making, having totally forgotten and displaced his Origins in Spirit.

These two dreams have been referred to in the *Course* as a 'double shield of oblivion', and were set up to make 'doubly' sure that we stayed in the ego's thought system. Since we remember nothing else, the totalitarian ego thought system successfully established itself as supreme ruler, and we have been duped into believing that its uncontested image of reality is authentic.

These points about our beginnings have been brought up frequently because it is essential to comprehend the reasons for our recurring problems in this world. With our new found awareness, our purpose is to rise above the illusion and dismiss the repeat performances of an old and tired script.

We now understand that the secret dream gave rise to the world's dream that acts as a protective cover-up. If we dwell in the world's dream then, we never confront our guilt because it remains so deeply buried that we are not aware of its presence.

The first, or secret dream continues to remain repressed as we continuously project the guilt of the separation *from* the secret dream *into* the world's dream and *then* onto others who appear to take part in this illusory scenario. This process happens so fast that it appears to be instantaneous, and since it is subconscious, we are not aware of it taking place at all. Only as we work backwards through the world's dream and realize its vacuous nature, can we begin to confront this frightening secret dream and realize that it has no power.

We believe that we are awake in the physical world but we are in actuality only dreaming a dream of a world under blanketing layers of forgetfulness. The Holy Spirit's agenda is to help us to remember our rightful Inheritance.

The purpose of the ego's world dream is to take all of the sins that we believe we have committed and keep them securely locked away as real crimes, and then they will be periodically aired out to convict us of our guilt. Since these secret thoughts of guilt are locked away, they can't be confronted and will remain securely tucked away under the ego's despotic authority. Now, since the ego is in charge, it will decide when they should be trotted out to be used against us.

If we follow this sequence of events, it leads to the inevitable conclusion that the world itself was projected out to veil over the secret dream's hidden agenda that keeps the guilt of the separation thought in place. We can therefore deduce that *anything* that is done in the world of 'effects' will avail us nothing because it is not the source of the problem. It becomes a fundamental necessity to bypass the illusory world and all of its distractions and realize that our *only* problem is the false belief that the separation was possible and a reality, and this has led us to the false image that the ego wants us to keep; of a Father that is a tyrannical ruler to be feared.

Since at this point we believe that the world's dream is real, let us recognize that as a consequence of this belief we are interpreting all events and circumstances within the parameters of the ego's thought system. The emotional investment that we have in the outcome of events is therefore extremely strong and is taken very seriously.

In the past, we may have tried to get rid of any feelings of uncertainty or hostility by trying to ignore or cast them from our awareness or by doing something behaviorally to ease our guilt. Since ideas do not leave their source, in this case the source is the ego's self-contained thought system, these thoughts cannot be driven out by denying them or wishing them away, or trying to eliminate them in the world of effects. We will only be able to overcome this dilemma by going 'outside of the box' of the ego's thought system and seeing with the Holy Spirit's eyes.

With the Holy Spirit's help, this churning mass of ego thoughts can be confronted and seen for what they are. If they are not dealt with, held onto or ignored, the guilt and fear must and *will* seep out of the recesses of our subconscious into our world in a multitude of ways, and that guilt will taint *everything* that we see and experience. We cannot pretend that they don't exist or escape them by denying that they are there.

With the *Course's* aid, we are now aware that all of our guilt and fear lies in the repository of the secret dream and it is the subconscious motivating factor for all of the thoughts and actions in this / our world. As we realize that the secret dream is the physical worlds' causative agent, we have to work 'backwards' from our awareness in this world to release the guilt for what has not happened and effectively remove the obstacles, block by block from our consciousness. We will then find ourselves once again standing in the doorway to the Home that we never left.

The Text reveals in the following the subconscious cause of our pain;

Here is the cause of suffering, (the secret dream) the space between your little dreams and your reality. The little gap you do not even see, the birthplace of illusions and of fear, the time of terror and of ancient hate, the instant of disaster, all are here. Here is the cause of unreality. And it is here that it will be undone.[1]

Again, the *cause* of our misery and fear is the subconscious secret dream, where fear was born and where it festers unacknowledged. The ego wants the secret dream kept in place so that we will not confront its unreality. The ego further protects itself by producing the *second* dream thought, and it is in this world of effects that we find ourselves.

Now we understand how the secret dream and the world's dream are inextricably linked. The first dream is the cause or reason that the world was made, and the second dream is the product or effect, and is the purpose for the world's existence.

The following idea is a subtle aspect of the world's dream, and the objective is to drape another opaque veil over our mind to obscure the recognition of our True Self. This is always the goal of all of the ego's ideas, but this particular distortion's purpose is to solidify our belief that the waking state that we experience in the world is the only reality.

As we perceive the world, what we are really seeing is the ego's secret dream out-pictured within the dream of a world, and this produces an inaccurate conviction that this concrete world is authentic. This perception is further reinforced as we appear to experience two states in the world, a dream state and a waking state.

Presently, we consider our waking state to be a tangible reality and our dreaming state as a jumbled mixture of unconscious desires and fears. We experience our waking life and our dream state side by side and imagine that there is a difference, but they are really comprised of different components of the same dream.

In this scenario, as we experience the world's dream as our waking state, we confuse being awake in the world with our True Life. We live out our lives, and while we are 'awake' we struggle to try find meaning and a purpose to our lives, but do not realize that we are only sleeping and dreaming of events. As we wander from place to place we are, unbeknownst to us, rumbling around in an illusion that is going nowhere. We are tricked into thinking that this world is real as it presents us with a virtual reality containing all of the pleasures and pains of life. Does it not prove to us that the world is a reality since we 'wake up' in it every day? We are lulled into an acceptance of our lot in life that seeks no further for the Truth. All the while, even though we are unaware of it, we are residing peacefully outside of time and space in our Father's tranquil embrace. Now our goal becomes to be conscious of it.

To summarize then, the ego set up a facsimile of the real world by contrasting our waking state with our sleeping state, so that we would believe that one is reality and the other a dream. With this deception in place, we believe that the dreaming of our sleeping state occurs within a world of 'reality', never to be aware that we are so much more.

Since we are ensconced in the ego world, this previous mindset produces a subliminal uncertainty. As of now the Holy Spirit's realm is invisible to us, leading us to fearfully question the Holy Spirit's thought system, and wonder if it is possibly *not* the truth? This anxiety seems legitimate since we have made the invisible (illusion) real, and have rejected the Visible (Spirit) from our sight. We fear that if we looked into that now unseen realm, we would gaze upon nothing, or our annihilation. Because of this frightful misperception, we hurriedly cast our eyes downward, and are in a panic to once again be with our familiar, albeit dismal ego friends of sin, doubt, guilt and fear.

A logical progression of the preceding ideas is to realize that we can never understand any problem by looking for answers in the world's dream. The world's dream is comprised of wishful solutions to illusory problems. The world is an *effect* of the secret dream that makes every effort to remain hidden from our discovery. Not realizing this hitch, we have ineffectively persisted in looking to the effects of the world for solutions, and therefore have not seen the cause of those perceived problems. Until now this has been a successful ploy that has kept us from focusing on the only Answer to any problem.

It has been like we were looking into a mirror and banging on it trying to change the image that we perceived. What we want to do is penetrate the barriers that we have erected in our minds and understand the *cause* of our perceived problems. It is only then that we will no longer see something that is not there, and will no longer fight ineffectively against windmills as did Don Quixote.[2]

As we take these observations into account, we can see how self-sustaining and encapsulated the ego's world really is. The *Course* provides an alternative option that will open our eyes, and this revelatory decision lies in following the Holy Spirit. We now rely on Him to guide us and we know that we always can trust His Answer. His guidance will help us step outside of the dream where our True Self is revealed and the false self is exposed.

To Bring about Transformation
What we need to do to affect a real and lasting change is to transform our minds and alter our perspectives so that we can look squarely at the *cause* of the secret dream of this fearful world. To bring about this change, we begin by asking for assistance from the Holy Spirit. We ask Him to help us be aware of our thoughts as we move throughout our day so that we can then apply the principles of advanced forgiveness. (As we remember, advanced forgivingness is seeing beyond the physical error and not taking the dreaming world so seriously because we see all that transpires as either Love or a call for Love.) By following His lead, we can generalize these ideas to all the little (and big) irritations and upsets that plague us during our day, be it anxiety about being late for an appointment or being distraught by the

political climate of China.

How we perceive current events propels us into the thought system that we now can choose. It has been the unforgiving thought that has kept our fear in place and blocked our true vision to see beyond form. Now we are aware that it is important to be vigilant about our thoughts, assessing continually how we view people, circumstances and events. We must not berate ourselves if we find ourselves being judgmental, but only to be aware that we have been, and then choose differently. Let us realize that we are taking a huge step in our progress to be able to see our ego at work, for we previously had no idea that we were making a choice for an illusory mindset or that we were functioning within its limitations.

We can add one more idea from the Text that will help us perforate and deflate the entrenched ego thought system. Let us reconsider our new awareness that all of our positive or negative thinking, opinions, notions, loves and hates are an outer manifestation of the fearful secret dream. Although this secret dream is deeply buried in our subconscious, it is nonetheless out-pictured in a multitude of external ways in our lives.

If we take a look at the following excerpt we can gain an added understanding as to the manifestations of the secret dream and how it operates in the world we see.

'Yet what you see as gifts your brother offers represent the gifts you dream your Father gives to you.'[3]

This means that every thought that we have for or against our brother directly reflects through the candid eyes of the Holy Spirit the way we feel about our Father. The interpretation of what we see immediately reveals to our vigilant awareness any subconscious misperceptions that we hold against Him. If we judge, criticize and interpret events and circumstances negatively, it shows us what we believe has been done to us by our Father, as well as what we imagine we have 'wrested' from Him to gain and keep our individuality. Now we understand that *everything* that we perceive, every interaction and every interpretation of any event or circumstance, echoes what we *really* think on a subliminal level about our Father, and mirrors what motivates every facet of our sojourn here on earth. Every observation that we have is reduced to what our true feelings about God are. *We constantly reenact our unconscious relationship with our Father as we interrelate with our brother.* All interactions between our brother and ourselves exposes to our outer awareness the defensive wall that we had erected between ourselves and our Father as we tried to 'protect' ourselves.

Even though we have many loving thoughts in our relationships, (which is a positive step toward unification) we still all share in the secret foundational dream; there is the inevitable undercurrent of anxious thoughts that outwardly manifests in myriad ways. If we take things personally, and take offence and judge harshly, we keep the illusion of separation in place. The egos whole paradigm then becomes cemented into a perception of an 'external' manifestation. If we hold onto non-forgiveness in our relationships we keep the defensive line in place between our brother and ourselves (as well as between us and our Father), blindly believing and reinforcing the credo of 'them against us'.

Now if we realize that these images are an ego defense, we will come around full circle to heal the foundation upon which they were made. As we mend the relationships that we have with our brother (by being vigilant of our thoughts and forgive them in light of their non-reality), we thereby repair our relationship with our Father. We gladly understand that it was an irrational subconscious thought that stemmed from the secret dream which had given rise to all of our defenses.

As we gauge our thoughts and observe how they reveal which thought system we have ascribed to, we can extricate ourselves from the ego's nightmare and welcome with open arms the Holy Spirit's happy Alternative. We will notice that we are still dwelling within a dream world, but we are in a place where we are viewing all events, sights and sounds with the Holy Spirit's eyes. We will abide here for a while until our Father comes to lift us into His Everlasting Embrace. Now there is nothing that remains in the world that can take away our Peace, and there is nothing here that we do not look upon without the gentle light of understanding.

Again, since everything that happens here on the planet is a revolving drama of the original moment of terror when we decided to 'separate', all we have to do is pay attention to the way we perceive each other, and that illuminates a connecting link between this world and the secret dream from which everything has sprung. This path becomes, in Dr. Wapnick's words, 'The royal road that connects the world's dream to the secret dream, and will eventually lead us beyond it entirely.'4

As the secret dream is now exposed to our awareness, it can no longer hide from our discerning eye under layers of effluvia. As we have become more alert, we can immediately see whose hand we have and we will let Him guide us over the chasm back to the safety of our Redeemer. As we look at our now apparent thoughts and see the unmistakable evidence of where our choices have led us in the past, we will remake the only logical choice.

We have allowed our thoughts to dwell in darkness for far too long. It is time to take charge of our runaway thoughts and strive to reverse our thinking, for we are the only ones who can do it.

As Saying 59 says, we need to look to the Living One while we live, and as we live in this world we can surmount our fear and guilt to finally overcome it. We need to realize that:

God is not the author of fear, you are. You have chosen to create unlike Him, and have therefore made fear for yourself. You are not at peace because you are not fulfilling your function...Your ego has chosen to be afraid instead of meeting it (your function)...When you are afraid, be still and know that God is real, and you are His beloved Son in whom He is well pleased. Do not let your ego dispute this, because the ego cannot know what is as far beyond its reach as you are.[5]

Much of this hidden fear and guilt still affects our psyche, even if we are not consciously aware of the motivating factors behind our behaviors or our thinking. We do not need to be brought up in a formal religion to have these aforementioned constructs influence us. The ontological creation story is the backdrop for mankind's subconscious impetus regardless of race, religion or country.

We now have the understanding of how we have misperceived the world, and can recognize the buried reasons for that misunderstanding. We have gained a more complete picture of the foundation from which we and our brother operate. It becomes evident that these sublimated thoughts run our everyday lives and affect our relationships, views and family concepts. We now understand where anger, attack and fear erupt from.

If we can exchange our previously accepted viewpoints for those of the Holy Spirit's ideas, it can free us from any ambivalence we may have had about the role of God in our lives. In our mind God would no longer be misunderstood as being responsible for our unhappiness in this world (He is not punishing us, and we are not victims).

We are no longer chained to the concept of being a victim of an unloving God, and are no longer afraid of a vengeful God penalizing us for our perceived transgressions. As we take responsibility for our actions and change our choices, every experience that we have of our Father would *only* be of His unconditional and unlimited Love. We would come to realize He does not have a split nature that gives or takes on a whim, or metes out punishment or salvation according to sacrifice rendered or rituals performed. This concept relieves us of the unacknowledged fear of commending ourselves unequivocally to our Creator. We now know that we will not be annihilated for our perceived offenses but will be accepted with open arms and an open heart, even as the prodigal Son returned to his Father's joyful embrace.[6] Our trust in Him is now our refuge.

As a thought-provoking aside, the story of the return of the prodigal son to his loving father could be considered more of a parallel to the story of our beginnings and our objectives in this world then the traditionally accepted story of Adam and Eve's banishment from the Garden of Eden. The banishment that takes place because of 'sinful' actions reinforces the fear of the Father's vengeance and retribution, which we are now trying to overcome. The Garden of Eden story also correlates with the traditional views of punishment and fear of God. The following Saying supports this thought of our Father's absolute, unwavering Love.

Saying 107:
J said, 'God's Divine Rule is like a shepherd who had a hundred sheep. One of them, the largest, went astray. He left the ninety-nine and looked for the one until he found it. After he had toiled, he said to the sheep, 'I love you more than the ninety-nine.''

We see here again, that it is the prodigal son who had thought himself lost but has been found, and has come back to his 'right mind' to be swept up into his Father's embrace. As the Son comes back into the fold, he has finally seen that there was no 'sin of separation' but only an error in thought that has now been undone; he realizes that it was only his self-imposed exile that had kept him from his beloved Father. The circle of Oneness is now complete as his inherent Birthright is embraced.

When we are honest with ourselves as we look upon our

errors, and endeavor to see them with forgiving eyes, our True Inheritance will be revealed to our sight. We see that the thoughts and actions that were set into motion by us in the illusory world meant nothing and will fade away into insignificance before the inexpressible Light. We need to see the illusion for what it is while we are immersed in the dream, for only then can we transcend its unreality and free our mind.

It is important to be aware that there is an unacknowledged resistance to facing these fears. As we have mentioned, we have disclaimed and projected our fear out and have kept the illusion of separation in place. This denial of our Divine Birthright of Oneness comes from not only believing in the ego's lie of retribution, but also because we have accepted the ego as a friend who told us a story that this world is our only reality. We are so immersed in the belief of the 'reality' of the ego world that we are afraid to completely forsake it, for to change our concepts induces a fear that we will lose ourselves.

Therefore Jesus, who is quite aware of our concerns, lovingly guides us with measured steps to our Father's House. *A Course in Miracles* is his gift of loving understanding that will guide us at our own pace through the valley of shadows without fear or a sense of sacrifice. If we concede that we have forgotten our Divine estate, and do accept the thoughts of the Holy Spirit as Truth, the concepts that we had considered unassailable before would now come to be viewed as flimsy and illusory. We will never again take the world as seriously, for we will have seen that the ego's dream was the cause of all of our pain.

Our goals and purpose change to that of the single-minded pursuit of removing the obstacles that are between ourselves and God's Kingdom. Now our eternal joy can once again be embraced. The miracle has taken place when we recall that what we had perceived is not reality but only a laughable dream that was once taken seriously. Our will is recognized as His Will, and that we are forever One with our Father. All we need to do is ask, and Jesus and the Holy Spirit will offer us the help and support that we need to look at our fears and to face them squarely. With Their help we will undo the dream and see the ego and its world dispelled. The ego will disappear because its dream system no longer serves the purpose of keeping us 'walled-in' and 'protected'. Our eyes will open to see the eternal Love of our Father that has always been and will always be.

So, as we once again acknowledge our Reality, we see the 'effects' of this world and smile at their incapacity to disturb our Peace. We now realize more and more that all of our varied problems were just a camouflage for the real reason for our misery *and* our only problem, which was the seeming separation from God that we had made real.

This world is an out-picturing of an inward thought, and it is based on the secret dream. When we hunger, it is the subconscious desire to fill up on the Love of God. When we fear, it is because of our fears of a vengeful God, and we feel separate and alone. When we resist authority, we are resisting the merging of God into our lives and thereby proving the separation 'real'. When we are lonely and looking for a special relationship, it is the yearning to join with God. When we are hateful toward our brother, it is our distancing of ourselves from God and using our brother as a surrogate for the fear and guilt that we harbor against our Father.

We now understand that these attack thoughts are a silent call for the love that we all so desire. Even something as 'simple' as sadness or depression has the same foundation. The list is endless and has but one common denominator.

What is striking about *A Course in Miracles* is the enlightening discourse on all of the concepts that motivate us subconsciously. Once we are aware of these impulses, we are given the means and support to transcend them. With these tools we can now undertake the process of healing our relationship with our brother, and as we do so, we will find that we are healing our relationship with our Father. Our misperceived relationship with our Father has always been the only problem that has been out-pictured in the revelry of dreams.

Lesson Five in the Workbook summarizes this point very concisely, 'We are never upset for the reasons we think.' It is quite remarkable that everything we do, say or think has only *one* subconscious foundation, and that it is the cause of all of the effects that we perceive in the world.

To conclude our discussion of cause and effect, it becomes obvious to us that the answer to 'curing' the problem of the separation cannot be found in the world, as the world is the effect of the secret dream and is the starting place of the illusory problems that we all think we have, and we know that we cannot solve an illusion with another illusion.

We have to acknowledge the *cause* of the secret dream and look at it boldly with the Holy Spirit at our side. It is important to remember that as we dispassionately observe these circum-stances that there is nothing to fear, because *both* the secret dream and the world's dream are the Son's mental construct, and in reality we are resting in God.

One dream is buried deep within the other but they are occurring simultaneously. They are the cause and effect of the illusion, totally outside of the Oneness and Reality of God. They cannot converge with Truth because the dream of a world does not exist, and an illusion can have no tangible effects.

Recognizing What is Real
One of the main premises that *A Course in Miracles* relays is that there are two emotions, love and fear and the only one that is real is Love. Since fear is not real, being a product of the ego's made-up world, the only reality is the all encompassing Love of God that stands ever magnificent beyond the dream. The *Course* puts it beautifully;

Nothing real can be threatened.
Nothing unreal exists.
Herein lies the peace of God.[7]

We accept these Truths for ourselves by relying on the Holy Spirit's judgment and surrender our upside-down thinking. We realize more and more, as the obstacles to our Divinity fade away, that our brother has done nothing but dream, and operates out of fear to protect the 'little domain' that he thinks is reality, just as we had done. We understand that we are the same, and *what is the same is One*. Our brother has had the same illusory secret dreams of fear and death that we did, even though his fears may have manifested differently. What is the most important point to recognize is that we share the same magnificent Reality.

Again, let us keep in mind that we are striving to change our mental processes. We are not denying that there are violent acts that take place on this planet; Jesus even states in the Text of the *Course* that frightened people can do vicious things.

With this in mind though, we also realize that the acts that take place on the planet are an out-picturing on a mass scale of the insanity of the ego thought system. To deny the acts of physical or mental violence in the world would be foolish and is not the position of the *Course*. Our soul objective is to change our mind's perspective, then all else will then fall into place.

Know that even as cruel acts are done by those who are deeply asleep, it is possible to see our brother without judgment and interpret his actions differently. With our new-found outlook we are able to look past those provoking actions and recognize the underlying motivating factors that produced them. We see that he is silently calling for rescue from a nightmare that he cannot see beyond, and that within those actions is an unspoken appeal for forgiveness and understanding. Our vision changes as we understand our brother's plea, for we realize that our journey is the same. We recognize that these are not personal attacks against us, because we have *our* ego mind in check. With the Holy Spirit's aid, we are now aware that without us our brother would lose their way, and without them our way could never be found. Thus, together we become each other's savior.

Remember, since our brother is a reflection of our deep personal thoughts about our Father, he mirrors what we secretly believe about ourselves and God. Using this gauge then, we will endeavor to make that reflection an image of beauty, for only together can we walk as One unto our Father's Kingdom.

We have discovered that as we acknowledge the Christic Essence in our brothers, we recognize the Christ in ourselves.[8] As we see with the eyes of the Living One, we will witness the real world and have our glimpse of Heaven. As we let go of the errors of the ego thought system and begin to rely on the Holy Spirit's guidance, we find that His direction becomes a gentle 'undoing-in the sense that it does nothing, failing to support the world of dreams and malice. Thus it lets illusions go. By not supporting them, it merely lets them quietly go down to dust.'[9]

Let us not confuse the perception of the world as a defense with physical defense. The term 'defense' is used in the *Course* to outline the defensive thoughts that we ascribe to, not defenses that protect us physically in the world. The defensive thoughts that *A Course in Miracles* is referring to are those that have the purpose of keeping the Love of God away, and those that keep us in the perceived 'safety' of the ego's thought system.

We may ask, 'Why would we want to keep the Love of God away?' The answer to this question returns us again to the subconscious, imaginary fear that occurred when we listened to the ego. The ego told us that we would be destroyed, or at the very least punished for our sin of separation if we turned toward the Light. Since forgetfulness descended when we chose the ego's erroneous thought system, we inadvertently cut ourselves off from the Truth that depicts our Divine Reality.

Now with our new understanding, we can detach from the

world's ups and downs and not be tossed around from pillar to post. We are gently supported as we steadily cling to the solid rock of our Foundation and know that only this is Real. As we do this more and more in our everyday situations, the real world will open up and joy and peace will flood through the illusion and sweep away what never was.

It does not mean that we ignore situations that require our attention but we will be able to function in the world with a sure purpose and a sense of peace instead of operating from an illusory thought system where we constantly battle imaginary demons.

There is no need to fear that we are going to be propelled out of this world into the next without so much as a backward glance. Jesus offers us a gentle path, where we are led through this world to look upon all with joy and love. As our efforts come to fruition, we draw closer to the real world and our right mind where the Holy Spirit's thought system holds sway, and it is here that we will know that we have always existed within our Father's Heart.

We now embrace the *Courses'* guidelines for our freedom from illusions with this admonition;

Anger is *never* justified. Attack has *no* foundation. It is here escape from fear begins, and will be made complete. Here is the real world given in exchange for dreams for terror.[10]

If we succumb to anger or attack thoughts we make the mistake of listening to the ego's discordant voice and bind ourselves to delusion. Instead, let us free ourselves from those detrimental thoughts that inevitably come into our consciousness. First we look at them objectively, and then choose to dismiss their angry countenance.

Let us remember to: 'Release instead of bind, for thus are you made free. The way is simple. Every time you feel a stab of anger, realize you hold a sword above your head. And it will fall or be averted as you choose to be condemned or free.'[11]

This is a key idea in accepting our accountability for the dream and to firmly plant our feet on the road to salvation. We now accept the idea there is no one else to blame for the projections that we made during the dream of fragmentation. We have taken responsibility for our dream and turned toward our Creator. Our hearts are open to the Love of God because we have found that our errors and perceived sins have never been, and we know that we are loved unconditionally. There is only Love reflecting back our pure innocence and we merge once again into the Oneness that always was.

Now that we have done an in-depth study of the foundational teachings of Jesus from *A Course in Miracles*, we will not only parallel them with many of his parables from *The Gospel of Thomas*, but we also have the entire translation reproduced here. As we study these Sayings from our new perspectives, we will gain insights that will help us on our life's journey and open our hearts further to our Father's Love.

PART 2

Chapter One

Preamble to the Gospel

Before we go on, there are some significant points to mention in reference to this version of *The Gospel of Thomas*. Throughout this particular gospel, the letter 'J' was used instead of Jesus' full name. Over the centuries his original Hebrew name, Y'shua, was translated from Hebrew to Greek and then to English, so technically it should have been Jeshua, or even Joshua, but not Jesus. Therefore, he has been called 'J' throughout this text so that either name could be inferred.

One of the reasons this specific translation was chosen is because it has been made known that in the 300-400 years between the writing of *Thomas' Gospel* and the burying of this text found in 1945 that these Sayings had been tampered with and / or had information added onto the original writings. (See Appendix D) Revisions were made to this text so that the words of the Master would be conveyed and not the words of those who throughout history may not have understood their deeper meaning and thereby mistranslated the words or added their own interpretations.

Saying 114 from the Nag Hammadi text is a prime example of why certain Sayings were omitted from this gospel. It is not included here, but in essence says, 'You have to make a female into a male before she can enter the Kingdom'. This appears to be a later addition to the Nag Hammadi edition, for it is not consistent with Saying 22 or other Sayings which teach us to look toward our Unity of Spirit and not give such import to a bodily image. Significantly in Saying 22, Jesus points out that to enter the Kingdom, duality and multiplicity must merge into the Oneness of the Sonship that is beyond form and gender. Keeping the Oneness that we have been studying in mind, we can deduce that Jesus would not profess a need to change anyone's body into a specific form as a criterion to enter the Kingdom, for he knew that we, as the One Son of God in *Spirit* cannot be bound by either a male or female form, and in Truth are limitless. Even as we review Jesus' ministry we see that he accepted everyone as they were, regardless of gender or creed.

Let us bear in mind that the profound teachings of Jesus were so astute and filled with light from beyond this world that it would be difficult for the average person of the time to filter the Master's knowledge through their own level of understanding. We can see how the ideas of Jesus could have been distorted or misrepresented over the centuries. Notably, as we understand that Jesus expressed love, and only love, his words and works would demonstrate only the fullness of these truths. It is evident that anything else could only be a misunderstanding of his message.

Combined with the teachings of our source books, we discover a deeper understanding of *Pursah's Gospel of Thomas*, and find in it's edited version a parallel to ageless teachings that are beyond traditional thought, expanding our awareness to seek and ultimately find, the 'Peace that passeth all understanding.'[1]

It is now my great joy to share this rendition of the timeless Sayings from this *Gospel of Thomas*.

Pursah's Gospel of Thomas

These are the hidden sayings that the living J spoke and Didymus Judas Thomas recorded:

1. (1) And he said, 'Whoever discovers the interpretation of these sayings will not taste death.'

2. (2) J said, 'Those who seek should not stop seeking until they find. When they find, they will be disturbed. When they are disturbed, they will marvel and they will reign over all.'

3. (3) J said, 'If your teachers say to you, 'Look, God's Divine Rule is in the sky,' then the birds will precede you. If they say to you, 'It's in the sea,' then the fish will precede you. Rather, God's Divine rule is within you and you are everywhere. When you know yourself, you will be known, and you will understand that we are one. But if you don't know yourself, you live in poverty, and you are the poverty.'

4. (4) J said, 'The person old in days should not hesitate to ask a little child the meaning of life, and that person will live. For many of the first will be last, and they will become a single one.'

5. (5) Know what is in front of your face, and what is hidden from you will be disclosed to you. For there is nothing hidden that will not be revealed.

6. (6) The disciples asked him, 'Do you want us to fast? How should we pray? Should we give to charity? What diet should we observe?' J said, 'When you go into any region and walk in the countryside, and people take you in, eat what they serve you. After all, what goes into your mouth will not defile you; rather, it's what comes out of your mouth that will reveal you.'

8. (7) J said, 'A wise fisherman cast his net into the sea. When he drew it up it was full of little fish. Among them he discovered a large, fine fish. He threw all the little fish back into the sea, and he chose the large fish. Anyone here with two good ears should

listen.'

9. (8) J said, 'Look, the sower went out, took a handful of seeds, and scattered them. Some fell on the road, and the birds came and ate them. Others fell on the rocks, and didn't take root and didn't produce grain. Others fell on the thorns, and they choked the seed and the worms ate them. And others fell on good soil, and it produced a good crop; it yielded sixty per measure and one hundred twenty per measure.'

11. (9) The dead are not alive, and the living will not die.

13. (10) J said to the disciples, 'Compare me to something and tell me what I'm like.' Simon Peter said to him, 'You are like a just angel.' Matthew said to him, 'You are like a wisdom teacher.' Thomas said to him, 'Master my mouth is utterly unable to say what you are like.'

And he took him, and withdrew, and spoke three sayings to him. When Thomas came back to his friends, they asked him, 'What did J say to you?' Thomas said to them, 'If I tell you one of the sayings he spoke to me you will pick up rocks and stone me, and fire will come from the rocks and consume you.'

17. (11) J said, 'I will give you what no eye has seen, what no ear has heard, what no hand has touched, and what has not arisen in the human heart.'

18. (12) The followers said to J, 'Tell us how our end will be.' He said, 'Have you discovered the beginning, then, so that you are seeking the end? For where the beginning is, the end will be. Fortunate is the one who stands at the beginning: That one will know the end and will not taste death.'

20. (13) The disciples said to J, 'Tell us what God's Divine Rule is like.' He said to them, 'It's like a mustard seed. It's the smallest of all seeds, but when it falls on prepared soil, it produces a large plant and becomes a shelter for birds of the sky.'

22. (14) When you make the two into one, and when you make the inner like the outer and the outer like the inner, and the upper like the lower, and when you make male and female into

a single one, so the male will not be male and the female will not be female...then you will enter the Kingdom.

23. (15) I shall choose you, one from a thousand and two from ten thousand and they shall stand as a single one.

24. (16) The disciples said, 'Show us the place where you are, for we must seek it.' He said to them, 'Anyone here with two ears had better listen! There is light within a person of light, and it shines on the whole world. If it does not shine, it is dark.'

26. (17) You see the speck that is in your brother's eye, but you do not see the log that is in your own eye. When you take the log out of your own eye, then you will see clearly enough to take the speck out of your brother's eye.

28. (18) I stood in the world and found them all drunk, and I did not find any of them thirsty. They came into the world empty, and they seek to leave the world empty. But meanwhile they are drunk. When they shake off their wine, they will open their eyes.

31. (19) A prophet is not acceptable in his own town. A doctor does not heal those who know him.

32. (20) J said, 'A city built on a high hill and fortified cannot fall, nor can it be hidden.'

34. (21) J said, 'If a blind person leads a blind person, both of them will fall into a hole.'

36. (22) Do not worry, from morning to night and from night until morning, about what you will wear. The lilies neither toil nor spin.

37. (23) When you take your clothes off without guilt, and you put them under your feet like little children and trample them, then you will see the son of the living one and you will not be afraid.

40. (24) A grapevine has been planted outside of the Father, but since it is not strong, it will be pulled up by its roots and shall pass away.

41. (25) J said, 'Whoever has something in hand will be given more, and whoever has nothing will be deprived of even the little

they have.'

42. (26) Be passersby.

45. (27) Grapes are not harvested from thorn trees, nor are figs gathered from thistles.

47. (28) A person cannot mount two horses or bend two bows. And a servant cannot serve two masters, or that servant will honor the one and offend the other.

Nobody drinks aged wine and immediately wants to drink young wine. Young wine is not poured into old wineskins, or they might break, and aged wine is not poured into new wineskins, or it might spoil. An old patch is not sewn onto a new garment, since it would create a tear.

48. (29) J said, 'If two make peace with each other in a single house, they will say to the mountain, 'Move over here!' and it will move.'

49. (30) Fortunate are those who are alone and chosen, for you will find the Kingdom. For you have come from it, and you will return there again.

51. (31) The disciples said to him, 'When will the rest for the dead take place, and when will the new world come?' He said to them, 'What you are looking forward to has come, but you don't know it.'

52. (32) The disciples said to him, 'Twenty-four prophets have spoken in Israel, and they all spoke of you.' He said to them, 'You have disregarded the living one who is in your presence, and have spoken of the dead.'

54. (33) Fortunate are the poor, for yours is the Father's Kingdom.

56. (34) Whoever has come to understand this world has found merely a corpse, and whoever has discovered the corpse, of that one the world is no longer worthy.

57. (35) God's Divine Rule is like a person who has good seed. His rival came during the night and sowed weeds among the good seed. The person did not let the workers pull up the weeds,

but said to them, 'No, otherwise you might go to pull up the weeds and pull up the wheat along with them. For on the day of the harvest the weeds will be conspicuous, and will be pulled up and burned.'

58. (36) J said, 'Congratulations to the person who has forgiven and has found life.'

59. (37) Look to the living One as long as you live. Otherwise, when you die and then try to see the living One, you will be unable to see.

61. (38) I am the one who comes from what is whole. I was given from the things of my Father. Therefore, I say that if one is whole, one will be filled with light, but if one is divided, one will be filled with darkness.

62. (39) J said, 'I disclose my mysteries to those who are ready for my mysteries. Do not let your left hand know what your right hand is doing.'

63. (40) There was a rich person who had a great deal of money. He said, 'I shall invest my money so that I may sow, reap, plant, and fill my storehouses with produce, that I may lack nothing.' These were the things he was thinking in his heart, but that very night he died.

66. (41) J said, 'Show me the stone that the builders rejected. That is the keystone.'

67. (42) J said, 'Those who know all, but are lacking in themselves, are completely lacking.'

70. (43) J said, 'If you bring forth what is within you, what you have will save you. If you do not have that within you, what you do not have within you will kill you.'

72. (44) A person said to him, 'Tell my brothers to divide my father's possessions with me.' He said to the person, 'Brother, who made me a divider?' He turned to his disciples and said to them, 'I'm not a divider, am I?'

75. (45) J said, 'There are many standing at the door, but those who are alone will enter the bridal suite.'

76. (46) J said, 'God's Divine Rule is like a merchant who had a supply of merchandise and then found a pearl. That merchant was prudent; he sold the merchandise and bought the single pearl for himself. So also with you, seek the treasure that is unfailing, that is enduring, where no moth comes to eat and no worm destroys.'

79. (47) A woman in the crowd said to him, 'Lucky are the womb that bore you and the breasts that fed you.' He said to her, 'Lucky are those who have heard the word of the Father and have truly kept it. For there will be days when you will say, 'Lucky are the womb that has not conceived and the breasts that have not given milk.'

80. (48) J said, 'Whoever has come to know the world has discovered the body, and whoever has discovered the body, of that one the world is not worthy.'

85. (49) J said, 'Adam came from great power and great wealth, but he was not worthy of you. For had he been worthy, he would not have tasted death.'

86. (50) J said, 'Foxes have their dens and birds have their nests, but human beings have no place to lay down and rest.'

87. (51) J said, 'How miserable is the body that depends on a body, and how miserable is the soul that depends on these two.'

88. (52) J said, 'The messengers and the prophets will come to you and give you what belongs to you. You, in turn, give them what you have, and say to yourselves, 'When will they come and take what belongs to them?''

89. (53) J said, 'Why do you wash the outside of the cup? Don't you understand that the one who made the inside is also the one who made the outside?'

90. (54) J said, 'Come to me, for my yoke is comfortable and my lordship is gentle, and you will find rest for yourselves.'

91. (55) They said to him, 'Tell us who you are so that we may believe in you.' He said to them, 'You examine the face of Heaven and earth, but you have not come to know the one who is in your

presence, and you do not know how to examine the present moment.'

92. (56) J said, 'Seek and you will find. In the past, however, I did not tell you the things about which you asked me then. Now I am willing to tell them, but you are not seeking them.'

94. (57) J said, 'One who seeks will find. And for one who knocks, it shall be opened.'

95. (58) J said, 'If you have money, do not lend it at interest. Rather, give it to someone who will not pay you back.'

96. (59) J said, 'God's Divine Rule is like a woman. She took a little leaven, hid it in dough, and made it into large loaves of bread. Anyone here with two ears had better listen!'

97. (60) J said, 'God's Divine Rule is like a woman who was carrying a jar full of meal. While she was walking along a distant road, the handle of the jar broke, and the meal spilled behind her along the road. She didn't know it; she hadn't noticed a problem. When she reached her house, she put the jar down and discovered it was empty.'

99. (61) The disciples said to him, 'Your brothers and your mother are standing outside.' He said to them, 'Those here who do what my Father wants are my brothers and my mother. They are the ones who will enter the Father's Kingdom.'

100. (62) They showed J a gold coin and said to him, 'The Roman Emperor's people demand taxes from us.' He said to them, 'Give the Emperor what belongs to the Emperor. Give God what belongs to God.'

103. (63) J said, 'Congratulations to those who know where the rebels are going to attack. They can get going, collect their Divine resources, and be prepared before the rebels arrive.'

106. (64) J said, 'When you make the two into one, you will become children of Adam, and when you say, 'Mountain, move from here!' it will move.'

107. (65) J said, 'God's Divine Rule is like a shepherd who had a hundred sheep. One of them, the largest, went astray. He left

the ninety-nine and looked for the one until he found it. After he had toiled, he said to the sheep, 'I love you more than the ninety-nine."

108. (66) J said, 'Whoever drinks from my mouth shall become like me. I myself shall become that person, and the hidden things will be revealed to that person.'

109. (67) J said, 'God's Divine Rule is like a person who had a treasure hidden in his field but did not know it. And when he died he left it to his son. The son did not know about it either. He took over the field and sold it. The buyer went plowing, discovered the treasure and began to lend money at interest to whomever he wished.'

110. (68) J said, 'Let one who has found the world, and has become wealthy, renounce the world.'

111. (69) J said, 'The Heavens and the earth will roll up in your presence, and whoever is living with the living one will not see death. Did not I say, 'Those who have found themselves, of them the world is not worthy'?'

113. (70) The disciples said to him, 'When will the Kingdom come?' He said, 'It will not come by watching for it. It will not be said, 'Behold here,' or 'Behold there.' Rather, the Kingdom of the Father is spread out upon the earth, and people do not see it.'

Chapter Two

Libretto

We have interspersed some foundational ideas throughout the following segments from *A Course in Miracles* that will give us an intriguing perspective on the teachings of Jesus. Many of the ideas that we have already discussed in the previous sections are reiterated throughout these commentaries, and now we will be able to ascertain their inter-relatedness. When we take them to heart, a new horizon of exciting possibilities opens up before us. These ideas will enable us to understand the function and purpose of our lives and help us to remove the blocks to our true vision. We will not only gain a fuller understanding of this gospel but will come to appreciate why it is in our best interest to make another choice than we have in the past.

As we can see, many of the teachings that are in the New Testament are also found here. What is unique about this gospel is that the Sayings are gathered together in one text and are giving a unified message.

Now, as one looks at this revised edition one can see that Jesus speaks consistently throughout these parables of Our Oneness with our Father, Oneness that is ours but which we cannot see or accept as yet. He is very aware of our struggles with our lower instincts, and repeatedly brings up the contrasts between our Higher and lower nature for our review so that we can make another choice.

With the new awareness of our Higher Self that is One with Him, let us gladly proclaim that; 'We are one because each part contains Your memory, and (therefore) truth must shine in all of us as one.'[2]

These are the hidden sayings that the living J spoke and Didymus Judas Thomas recorded.

Saying 1.

And he said, 'Whoever discovers the interpretation of these sayings will not taste death.'

'Didymus', which means twin in Greek, was included in the original introduction to *Thomas' Gospel* so that we would know who scribed the Sayings. The word 'hidden' does not refer to hiding anything, but refers to Jesus speaking many of the Sayings to a small group of people or in private.

To review a few of the precepts from Part One, in the *Course* Jesus explains that we have the ability to make a choice, one for the Holy Spirit's 'right mind' or for the ego's dysfunctional, judgmental 'wrong mind'. The decision making mind that makes those choices is the 'you' that the *Course* addresses. It is important to remember that this is not the mind that we identify with our body and brain, but the entire Mind outside of time, space, and form where we are joined as One, and where we are also eternally joined with the Holy Spirit and Jesus.

This Mind has the power to make the choice between the true and false thought systems and it directs our thoughts here in the world. The Holy Spirit is the connecting link between this Mind and who we perceive ourselves to be in the world. He is the connection that we hold onto and follow Home. As we view events in the world and observe them with Love and non-judgment, we can be confident that we are holding the Holy Spirit's hand. When we see the ego in action we will make the obvious choice for another Teacher, and this is the beginning of the end of the ego thought system.

We only need a small willingness[3] to learn to reinterpret our thoughts and we will find that by continually making this right minded choice, Jesus will lead us to the resurrection of our mind.

This definition of resurrection has nothing to do with the body but is an awakening from the mind's dream of despair to the real world that sees only joy and love.

As we remember, the real world that our eyes will one day light upon is defined as being the 'state of mind in which, through total forgiveness, the world of perception is released from the projection of guilt we had placed upon it: thus, it is the mind that has changed, *not the world*. We see with the vision of Christ which blesses rather than condemns...undoing our thoughts of separation and allowing God to take the last step.'[4] The real world is seen when we have dispelled guilt from our minds by advanced forgiveness and our vision has become purified to see all inside the circle of Atonement.

To expand upon the picture of the real world, the *Course* explains: 'The real world was given you by God in loving exchange for the world you made and the world you see...Its reality will make everything else invisible, for beholding it is total perception.'[5]

As our minds change, we rise above the chaos and look down upon a crystalline world purified by the Holy Spirit's vision of Truth. This has been accomplished by our consistently giving all of our illusions and judgments of ourselves and our brothers to the Holy Spirit. *A Course in Miracles* explains the idea of the pure vision of forgiveness that will lead us to the understanding of the non-duality of God's Oneness:

Forgive the world, and you will understand that everything that God created cannot have an end, and nothing He did not create is real. In this one sentence is our course explained...And in this one sentence is the Holy Spirit's whole curriculum specified exactly as it is.[6]

In seeing the real world, we have accepted the Holy Spirit's interpretation of the world's purpose, where we extend forgiveness and the Love of God to our brothers in genuine communication. This is truly living and ends the dreams of misery and despair, for our minds have been resurrected and unified.

It is then that 'one will not taste death', for one has found the true interpretation of the Sayings which proclaim the eternal truth of our Oneness with our Creator, and it is what we have wholeheartedly accepted as our own. It is within this Oneness that death cannot touch us at all, for it is only here where we can truly live. It is the recognition of the gifts of God, where 'Vision is wholly corrected and all mistakes undone ... (and) it is the single desire of the Son for the Father.'[7] Further, we understand that, 'God is. And in Him all created things must be eternal.'[8] This is the Mind identification that Jesus exemplified and sought to teach.

Saying 2:
> J said, 'Those who seek should not stop seeking until they find. When they find, they will be disturbed. When they are disturbed, they will marvel and they will reign over all.'

It is an innate goal to search for our God Reality, a deep subconscious need to find our Home, much to the chagrin of the ego mind, which will erect as many road blocks and temptations to keep us tethered to its dream. Nevertheless, when we do find our way on the spiritual path and set our sights upon the goal, our salvation is sure.

This Saying indicates that while we have placed obstacles in our own way, when those obstructions are exposed we will at first be disturbed. We will become aware that the past thoughts that we had ascribed to belonged to the ego's world and have been a chain and shackle of our own making. We will marvel over the fact that we had impeded our own progress, and were responsible for placing the stumbling stones of non-forgiveness in our own way. When this conundrum is exposed, and our goal is clear and our function apparent, there is no imaginary obstruction in this world that can stop our forward progression in attaining our salvation.

It is important to acknowledge that we are responsible for our interpretation of what we perceive. We have placed our thoughts and judgments upon the world, and that world mirrors our own state of mind. If we see a world in a state of fear, it is a reflection of what is within. If our thoughts abound with peace and forgiveness, our eyes see a world of purity and wholeness. We will marvel over the realization that the magnificent world of Peace was there all the time but we just did not see it. The following Text is from the *Course*, where Jesus helps us to take a good look at our handiwork, and how we can unravel it.

This is the only thing that you need do for vision, happiness, release from pain and the complete escape from sin, all to be given you. Say only this, but mean it with no reservations, for here the power of salvation lies:

I **am** responsible for what I see.
I choose the feelings I experience, and I decide
Upon the goal I would achieve.
And everything that seems to happen to me I ask for, and receive as I have asked.
Deceive yourself no longer that you are helpless in the face of what is done to you. Acknowledge but that you have been mistaken, and all effects of your mistakes will disappear.[9]

From these passages it is inconceivable that the Son of God could be subject to the capriciousness of a world beyond his control. As we come to realize the reasons for our previous accepted mode of thinking, we will indeed marvel that we could have been so naïve. As this distinctive understanding of the power of the Holy Spirit floods our awareness, we claim our birthright and realize

our Oneness with our brother and therefore our Father.
This small willingness to acknowledge our own part in the
drama is the only gift we need give the Holy Spirit, for it is the
invitation to Holiness to step into our Temple. We are thus
making a statement to the Divine that we will take responsibility
for our thoughts, and as we do, we find this small offering is
returned to us magnified beyond measure.

Saying number 47:

A person cannot mount two horses or bend two bows. And a
servant cannot serve two masters, or that servant will honor
the one and offend the other.

This Saying supports the concept outlined in our source books
which addresses the two thought systems that we must choose
between, the changeless and eternal Reality of Spirit or the
fearful, unreal and ever-changing universe of the ego. This is a
central theme in Jesus' teaching, and *A Course in Miracles*
parallels the above Saying:

You cannot be faithful to two masters who ask conflicting
things of you. (You think you can)…deal with part of the truth
in one way, and in another way the other part. To fragment
truth is to destroy it by rendering it meaningless. Salvation
from separation would be complete, or will not be at all.[10]

This highlights the fact that the Holy Spirit and the ego are two
opposing thought systems that are mutually exclusive. If we
retain even a little fragment of an illusory thought, we consequently find ourselves completely immersed in the ego's
autonomous dream of guilt. The Truth of our Oneness with our
Father is our Reality, and *everything* else is false. To underscore
this noteworthy point, Jesus continues in the *Course*;

One illusion cherished and defended against the truth makes all truth meaningless and all illusions real. Such is the power of belief. It cannot compromise.[11]

Belief is what keeps a thought system in place. Demosthenes (384-322BC), a Greek orator and statesman accurately said that 'The easiest thing of all is to deceive one's self; for what a man wishes he generally believes to be true.' A belief in any aspect of the dream keeps us entangled in the web of our illusions, concealing the Truth from our awareness. When we withdraw our power of belief from the wrong mindset and its barrenness is exposed, our Reality can then shine forth. The Truth is everlasting and is eternally within us, it has only been our inaccurate beliefs that have masked its glory.

As we are an idea thought by God, it is impossible to be separate from our Source. We can believe in a dream of division but it does not change the fact that our Oneness is forever safeguarded in the loving Presence of God.

In the New Testament Jesus parallels this Saying by cautioning us that; 'No man can serve two masters: for either he will hate the one, and love the other: or else he will hold to the one, and despise the other. Ye cannot serve God and mammon.'[12]

Here Jesus speaks again of the split mind, and as long as we retain even one illusion as valuable, we will cast ourselves into the arms of the ego, cutting ourselves off from Heaven's touch. Jesus does show us how to 'serve only one master'. As we diligently practice with him and the Holy Spirit to see everything through the eyes of Truth and not of judgment, we slowly peel away the illusions we have super-imposed upon our spiritual sight. We now begin to witness our True Reality beyond form.

We know that when we look at our brother critically we are in the ego's thought system. As we pause to consider that the ego is not the frame of mind that we want for ourselves, we make the determination to see all in the Light of God by propelling ourselves into the right minded thought system. The *Course* gives a helpful suggestion as to how to practice seeing our brother differently:

Weave...a frame of holiness around him, that the truth may shine on him, and give *you* safety from decay.[13]

Again, as we extend this Truth to our previous assessment of our brother, our thinking is slowly converted to the recognition of the Truth about ourselves. As the day follows the night, it is inevitable that the previous assessment of ourselves will change as we view our brother differently.

The Workbook of the *Course* continues to instruct us in the transformation of our vision to see our brother in a different light. In the schoolroom of life we need to keep the function of advanced forgiveness in the forefront of our mind.

There are obviously encounters with our brother that are forgiveness opportunities, and we deal with them in love. We also find in our day to day encounters that we will have many wonderful interchanges with our brother which mirror our Father's Loving glance. We are gladdened as we see our brother's smile reflecting our Father's Love for His Son, and we realize that there is nothing that he has received that is not our just due as well. We offer gratitude to our brother as his loving actions point the way to the remembrance of our Creator. This exchange of giving and receiving are symbols in the world of form of the treasure from the storehouse of our Father's Love, enabling us to see *everything* as being touched by the Loving Hand of God.[14] As we observe how the principles of these teachings apply to every aspect of our thinking, they make it possible for us to continually stand in God's radiance.

As we come back to Saying 47, we find that there are additional references that speak of this important premise of our inability to serve two masters. The Text of *A Course in Miracles* states;

Whatever is true is eternal, and cannot change or be changed. Spirit is therefore unalterable because it is already perfect, but the mind can elect what it chooses to serve. The only limit put on its choice is that it cannot serve two masters...To change your mind (to that of the Holy Spirit) means to place it at the disposal of *true* Authority.[15]

Placing our minds at the disposal of true Authority can be delayed, turned away from, or ignored, but ultimately this choice for God comes in time to every mind and will be embraced, for our heart's true desire will be made manifest.

As we can see, becoming aware of our inherent Oneness and the healing of our split mind is the prevalent theme stressed in this Saying, as well as throughout this gospel and in *A Course in Miracles*. To heal the rift takes effort and focus. The rewards are profound for those who endeavor to unify the Mind, as it will propel the seeker to heights of exhilaration undreamed of in this mortal world.

Saying 61:
I am the one who comes from what is whole. I was given from the things of my Father. Therefore, I say that if one is whole, one will be filled with light, but if one is divided, one will be filled with darkness.

As is indicated in this Saying, Jesus comes from what is whole and has recognized his Source. For us to regain the awareness of that same wholeness we must commit to recovering our divine heritage, and follow Jesus' example by being mindful that our thoughts are in alignment with the Truth. As the previous Saying indicated, we are divided if we retain even a small belief in a portion of the dream. As we allow a little bit of darkness and illusion into our consciousness, we fully step into the ego's world.

Vigilance for the condition of the Kingdom is mandatory[16] for our tendency is to follow the ego's divisive dictates of criticism and judgment. When we are vigilant and keep our center of attention on the Truth, we can catch the ego as it testifies to the wrong mind, and then ask the Holy Spirit to show us how to transform our thoughts into those of forgiveness and healing. When we are counseled to bring illusions to the Truth, it means that we are to bring all of the images, events and thoughts that parade across our mind to the Holy Spirit as they transpire. He will gently remind us again that *everything* that we perceive and react to in the world of form are misdirected thoughts that we have occupied ourselves with and given credibility to.

Again, the process of undoing our denial and dissociation is achieved by bringing the darkness (guilt and illusions) to the Light (awareness and Love) of the Holy Spirit to be looked at and forgiven rather than fearfully keeping the illusions in the darkness of our unconscious minds never to be seen or undone.[17] As we have Jesus by our side, we can look at our 'darkness' squarely without a sense of censure or shame. We have the confidence that those errors are dismissed as inconsequential by the all-encompassing Love of the Father Who knows His Son.

A Course in Miracles gives us a message to consider as we bring illusions to the Truth;

What seems to die has but been misperceived and carried to illusion. Now it becomes your task to let the illusion be carried to the truth. Be steadfast but in this; be not deceived by the 'reality' of any changing form.[18]

It would behoove us to ponder what our conception is of 'any changing form'. *A Course in Miracles* speaks of the Holy Spirit as the only Truth that is in our minds *and* in our brothers' mind. This Truth extends from the realm of Spirit and through all limited forms of this world to join us together in Oneness:

The Holy Spirit is in both your minds, and He is One because there is no gap that separates His Oneness from Itself. The gap between your bodies' matters not, for what is joined in Him is always One.

And:

Love knows no bodies, and reaches to everything created like itself. Its total lack of limit *is* its meaning. It is completely impartial in its giving...[19]

These are the minds that are joined beyond form in the limitlessness of Truth and Spirit and perceive Reality with the Holy Spirit's Vision. These minds are joined as One, and embody the Love that forgives ceaselessly. They have the sure knowledge of the Father's Will as their own and are therefore filled with Light.

Saying 72:
A person said to him, 'Tell my brothers to divide my father's possessions with me.' He said to the person, 'Brother, who made me a divider?' He turned to his disciples and said to them, 'I'm not a divider, am I?'

Here, as in the previous Saying, Jesus is focusing on the subject of division. He is saying that our Father does not know of division, for He is perfect Wholeness. Jesus as a manifestation of God's awakened Son does not give division credibility either, because he understands that God's Son is unified. He constantly challenges the thought system of the disciples as he asks them if they recognize the difference between being separate and being whole.

Jesus' intention is to help us see the deeper meanings of his parables that show us that we are already 'saved' and unified as One Son outside of time and space. He reveals how we are stubbornly clinging to the dream of our erroneous thoughts, and he discloses how we can loosen the iron grip with which we grasp them. When we call to him he will assist us in our efforts to remove the obstacles that are keeping us from remembering God's Love. He will show us how to use the forgiveness principles so that we may once more be undivided in the Thought of our Oneness with our Source.

Saying 108:

> Whoever drinks from my mouth shall become like me. I myself shall become that person, and the hidden things will be revealed to that person.

Jesus is speaking about a metaphysical joining here, where we are literally immersed in his awareness. This happens as we imbibe Jesus' thoughts and merge with his recognition of God in ourselves and our brothers. As we gaze upon our brothers as he did, with love and forgiveness, the Great Rays[20] extend through us and overlook the form to see only the content.

An allegory to this thought would be to look at a beautiful painting set in an ornate frame. We would see the exquisite detail and love of the subject matter in the painting and would realize that the frame, no matter how elaborate, is nothing in comparison with the painting, and actually detracts from the beautiful content of the picture. We find that the painting is all we desire to gaze upon and only this do we want to make our own.[21] So too is the content of God's essence residing within each and every one, blazing as a beacon in the night waiting in infinite patience to be recognized.

To shift our thoughts to those of Jesus, we need to acknowledge and accept the Holy Spirit's thought system and choose it consistently, then will our peaceful eyes light with compassion upon our brother. We will view all things as Jesus did, having accepted his message and thoughts as our own. The

Peace of God is transferred from one to the other to proclaim our holy innocence and Divine Unity. Our eyes light upon a different world, for our minds are One. *A Course in Miracles* says:

> Our emphasis is not on giving up the world, but exchanging it for what is far more satisfying, filled with joy and capable of offering you peace.[22]

The above statement reflects the thought of the real world that we are striving for, where we take on the garments of the Master and become like him to dwell in a world without the thoughts of sin, guilt or fear. The Son has overcome the old world, and in fact that world is no longer perceived. His wakened eyes comprehend the sure reflection of his Father's Love that surrounds him, and he has the faith in his Father's promise that he is redeemed.[23]

Jesus asks us to look at the ego's judgmental thoughts and review them objectively. We are *not* asked to give up or sacrifice anything. Eventually, as we look at all events in this objective manner, with the Love of the Holy Spirit at our side, we will find that the judgment that kept our guilt in place will fade away as we gently look upon events and circumstances with forgiving eyes. Our interpretations of our circumstances will take on new meaning as we look upon the exact same events without upset, and we see the real world with the clear vision that is devoid of fear, anger, or frustration.

Of course, we do not deny the suffering we observe in this world, but we find that our perception has changed as our minds have been enlightened. The appearance of suffering can no longer displace our mind's peace, or our conviction of our Wholeness that is beyond form. We now come from a place of holiness beyond this world that lovingly ministers to the pain our brothers suffer in the dream of separation, doing what we can in the world to alleviate the pain but are not deceived by it. As we do so, we strengthen our knowledge *and* our brother's confidence that our mutual Identity is not of this world.

Saying 23:
I shall choose you, one from a thousand and two from ten thousand, and they shall stand as a single one.

As Jesus speaks of choosing out of a multitude, we must realize that we are already chosen and do stand as a single one, but haven't the spiritual vision to see that it is so. It *is* Our Father's Will and therefore inevitable that God's Son will one day stand cognizant of his wholeness, for that *is* who he is.

It is not necessary to call outside of ourselves to bring the Light of God into our lives, for the light of our Oneness and Love are already contained within, albeit unacknowledged. The barriers that we have set up between ourselves and this knowledge are what we need to remove. As the Light of our Divinity is already within, we will come to realize that we have made a mistake by looking outward for salvation. We will see that it has always been shimmering on the outskirts of our perception just waiting to be recognized. As we step back and let it flow out, it will blossom to enfold the world.

Standing 'as a single one' becomes a reality as we acknowledge the ever-present light within. This is reiterated by the following quote from the *Course*: 'Why wait for Heaven? Those who seek the light are merely covering their eyes. The light is in them now.'[24]

With the understanding that the Light is already within, the riddle of the Saying unfolds. Where 'a multitude stands as a single one', we come to understand that we are a 'single one' in Spirit, even though we seem to be standing amidst a multitude of forms. As Jesus' knowledge of our Oneness is disclosed, we can disseminate these mystical teachings for ourselves and endeavor to incorporate their wisdom into our lives. We now can make the choice to look beyond form and actions to the indwelling light that resides within our brother.

To help us do so, *A Course in Miracles* again reveals our true nature by clarifying the purpose of the Holy Spirit that dwells within our One mind:

> The Holy Spirit extends by recognizing Himself in every mind, and thus perceives them as one…Wherever He looks he sees Himself, and because He is united He offers the whole Kingdom always…The great peace of the Kingdom shines in your mind forever….[25]

By accepting these concepts, the heavy self-imposed veils of forgetfulness melt away as a fog in the morning light, and the Peace of God dawns upon our awakened minds.

Saying 5:
> Know what is in front of your face, and what is hidden from you will be disclosed to you. For there is nothing hidden that will not be revealed.

What we need to recognize is what is in front of our face is illusion and our eyes have perceived a world where the valueless has been deemed valuable.[26] Know that God's Kingdom, the valuable, which seems to be hidden from our sight, is a world that will be disclosed to us when we recognize the valuelessness of the illusory world. In other words, the illusion will be seen for what it is, and the Truth that seemed to be invisible will be revealed to our awareness.

When we discern that we made our world and have kept it in place by our belief in illusions and judgment, we realize that we have the ability to remake our world by shifting our thought system to the Holy Spirit's plan of forgiveness. At that point, a new world will open up and we will understand the Truth in this Saying where all will be disclosed and nothing will be hidden.

We have pointed out that one of the key methods used by the Holy Spirit to expand our awareness as to the unreality of illusions is to help us realize that we are accountable for our thoughts and actions. We cannot cast blame on anyone else for our circumstances.

The secret of salvation is but this: That you are doing this unto yourself. No matter what the form of the attack, this is still true. Whoever takes the role of enemy and of attacker, still this is the truth. Whatever seems to be the cause of any pain and suffering you feel, this is still true.[27]

As we endeavor to take responsibility for our circumstances, and extend forgiveness to all life, it frees us from the dream of guilt, sin and fear, and reveals the real world which seemed to be hidden. We realize that we have done nothing to forfeit our inheritance. It is the Father's great pleasure to give all of Heaven to His Son, He does but wait in infinite patience for the Son to open his eyes and comprehend that it was already his.

Saying 58:
J said, 'Congratulations to the person who has forgiven and has found life.'

This Saying is important to mention from the standpoint of understanding ourselves all the better. Everyone has a dualistic split mind. Everyone has the vicious ego. Everyone also, has the saving grace of the Holy Spirit indelibly imprinted in their mind that will lead them out of the chaos. With the help of the Holy Spirit we are able to look at the ego and observe its power-lessness, and see it is as a frightened mouse roaring at the universe, futilely ineffective.

As we view events with the Holy Spirit as our guide, our view of the world is no longer attack-defense, defense-attack.[28] Now the world is transformed into a classroom called 'Forgiveness 101'. Now we see myriad opportunities to activate this 'new' thought system and reinterpret our prior view of the world. As we move forward and take responsibility for our actions and thoughts, we find we are not victims of circumstance, but literally had created our world as we see it, and find that only *we* had deprived ourselves of the peace of God[29] and we are the only ones who can reinstitute it.

The only thing that gives the ego its seeming power is our belief, protection, and justification of it. It is the first voice of defense or attack to surge into our awareness when we come upon a potentially volatile situation. We can rest assured that this dissonant voice is always the wrong thought system.

The Holy Spirit's Voice does not oppose. He has the calm assurance of knowing the one true interpretation. As we look at the ego and its world with the discernment of Jesus and the Holy Spirit, the ego will be undone. As the ego is not supported any longer by judgment or attack thoughts,[30] it withers away and leaves the sparkling essence of the real world of forgiveness and peace in its place.

The following excerpt details the *Course's* thought system on forgiveness of our brother, giving us an understanding of the Holy Spirit's definition of forgiveness that sees beyond the physical realm.

Forgiveness takes away what stands between your brother and yourself. It is the wish that you be joined with him, and not apart....it does remove the obstacles you have placed between the Heaven where you are, and the recognition of where and what you are.[31]

Forgiveness removes the barriers that we have placed between our brother and ourselves. Those obstacles are the beliefs in separation and differences, and once we recognize that we are

One in Reality our eyes will be open to the Truth and see it every-where. Any of these self-imposed obstructions have limited our vision to see only separated bodies and objects, instead of our Oneness as Spirit.

Again, this is the result of the original ontological separation, and reflects the subconscious wish to *be* apart. This wish is what forgiveness removes, replacing fear with the joyful recognition and true understanding that we are forever joined in thought beyond form. As we heal the fissure between our brother and ourselves, we take the first steps in healing the separation that we had thought occurred between ourselves and our Father all that time ago. Now with our new awareness we are that much closer to our joyful reunion.

We only made an error of transposing our thoughts of fear of our Father onto our brother because we believed that this substitution was an easier idea to control. As we reverse this projection and correct it, we can respond to the Loving Embrace that always has nurtured us. With these thoughts in mind, we can accept the following important point:

Ideas are of the mind. What is projected out, and seems to be external to the mind, is not outside at all, but an effect of what is in, and has not left its source....[32]

This idea is a major principle of *A Course in Miracles*. If we keep this tenet in mind as we look upon the world, we will realize that what we had seen were the blocks and fears that we had suppressed. We humbly recognize that we had projected the fear and guilt outward but it has never left our mind.

Let us now initiate the process of looking within, and make the choice to see the unconditional Love that flows continually from the Fount of Life and then extend it to all creation. Since we are of God's issue and He is our Source, we are like Him in every way and One with Him in awareness beyond all form. As He Is, so are we also.

Since this is so, then we must accept that this Truth cannot be overturned or replaced with any of our own self-concepts such as corruption, guilt, unworthiness, etc. Those illusory concepts are not and cannot be true as they are not of God. We have believed (dreamed) these concepts were components of our make-up but that idea remains an erroneous belief and does not change our Reality.

The Workbook offers us some transforming thought constructs for our consideration;

Perception is a mirror, not a fact. And what I look on is my state of mind, reflected outward. (My goal is to)...bless the world by looking on it with the eyes of Christ.[33] (i.e. the unified vision of the Christic Mind)

And also to remember;

Projection makes perception. The world you see is what you gave it, nothing more than that....It is the witness to your state of mind, the outside picture of an inward condition. As a man thinketh, so does he perceive. Therefore, seek not to change the world, but choose to change your mind about the world. Perception is a result and not a cause. And that is why order of difficulty in miracles is meaningless.[34]

It can appear that some illusions have more validity than others, but in reality illusion does not have any Truth within it because *all* illusions are based on a falsehood, and all conclusions within its parameters are erroneous. There can be no ranking (some better, some worse) of illusions because they are all unreal. This is the Truth. As the Text tells us;

All that must be forgiven are the illusions you have held

against your brothers. Their reality has no past, and only illusions can be forgiven. God holds nothing against anyone, for He is incapable of illusions of any kind. Release your brothers from the slavery of their illusions by forgiving them for the illusions you perceive in them. Thus will you learn that you have been forgiven...[35]

These illusions that stem from the ego mind, include how we perceive our brother's body and his behaviors, as well as the judgmental thoughts that we have about ourselves. Forgiveness removes this projection of guilt and fear of punishment from the Son's consciousness, so he can safely look beyond the physical realm and see all united in the Sonship of God. Now we can look to the light beyond the differences that appear to reflect separation and see wholeness mirrored back. A message of hope and redemption is given in the following passage.

What could you want forgiveness cannot give? Do you want peace? Forgiveness offers it. Do you want happiness, a quiet mind, a certainty of purpose, and a sense of worth and beauty that transcends the world? Do you want care and safety, and the warmth of sure protection always? Do you want a quietness that cannot be disturbed, a gentleness that never can be hurt, a deep abiding comfort, and a rest so perfect it can never be upset? All this forgiveness offers you and more. Why would you seek an answer other than the answer that will answer everything?[36]

Another gift forgiveness offers is that it 'lets the veil be lifted up that hides the face of Christ from those who look with unforgiving eyes upon the world. It lets you recognize the Son of God, and clears your memory of all dead thoughts so that remembrance of your Father can arise across the threshold of your mind.'[37]

Let us sweep the cobwebs away and let the Light stream through the windows of our Temple. We shall accomplish this task of embracing the Holy Spirit's thought system of forgiveness while we are still in this world, or, as the following Saying states, when we die we will be unable to see the Truth, for it will have been obscured from our sight once again.

Saying 59:

Look to the living One as long as you live. Otherwise, when you die and then try to see the living One, you will be unable to see.

The living One refers to the Holy Spirit, Who is the Voice for God. He addresses us in symbols, language, and images here in the world. 'We look to Him to attain our salvation while we are still seemingly in a body. If we don't, we won't find enlightenment somewhere on the other side afterwards...Heaven is not a reward that is bestowed on us by an outside force for good behavior or clever metaphysical musings.'[38] As we hear his message, we can embrace our inheritance by our small willingness to find a better way. The only manner in which we can overcome the world as Jesus did[39] is to amend our thoughts to those of the Holy Spirit. It takes focus and effort to attain our hearts desire.

As we examine our beliefs about the events in our lives, we can use those tools to assist us in stepping back with the Holy Spirit to look at our thoughts objectively, and dismiss those thoughts that are not in alignment with Him. When we ask for the Holy Spirit's help; He will always remind us to see through the eyes of Truth and not of judgment, and continually remind us to look to forgiveness of ourselves and others.

We call to the Living One as the mediator between our Real Self and all illusions. He sees the illusion but knows the Truth of our Divinity. The world is where we have to ask for His help, because this is where our consciousness dwells and where we have made the mistakes in our choices and in our thoughts.

Saying 34:
   J said, 'If a blind person leads a blind person, both of them
   will fall into a hole.'

Jesus tells us in the *Course* to not ask the stranger (ego) for
guidance, for it is the one thing in the entire universe that does
not know the way of Truth. If we do ask the ego for direction, its
answer will lead us astray and we will fall deeper into the
illusion. The ego can only reinforce the dream state, and would
leave us to stumble around in the darkness of sightless misery.
When we are in its dark thought system of judgment and fear, we
are blinded to the pure vision of the Holy Spirit Who will give us
the one and only Answer that can bring Light into the darkness.
The Answer is the gentle reminder that what we have believed to
be true was a dream born of fear. The good news is that our fears
are unwarranted, the separation has not occurred, and we are
forever beloved of our Father.

   We have been hindered in the past by relying on false ideas,
only to find; 'our judgments (were) giving us false directions...
(While) true vision shows us where to go. Why should we
guess?'[40] This is a call to change our teacher to that of the Holy
Spirit. It is with a great sense of relief that we renounce our
judgments and false ideas and gladly hand them over to the
Holy Spirit where all of our previous assumptions evaporate.

   The following excerpt from the *Course's* Text tells us how we
have made a mistake in our choice of a teacher and have thereby
succumbed to the ego's sightless world.

   The blind become accustomed to the world by their adjust-
   ments to it. They think they know their way about in it. They
   learned it...through the stern necessity of limits they believed
   they could not overcome...they hold those lessons dear, and

cling to them because they cannot see. They do not understand the lessons *keep* them blind. This they do not believe.
And so they keep the world they learned to 'see' in their
imagination.[41]

Here again, the choice we have made as to what we want to see
is apparent. It shows us how we have clung to the precepts of the
world and believed that this is all there was.

The *Course* also points out that we don't realize that our
perception of the outer world is a product of our inner thoughts
projected out, and those projected images are only a distorted
'thought fragment' of the whole. The function of our physical
eyes is to see form and not beyond it. This 'sight' gives validity to
the projected images that we think we are seeing as well as to the
thoughts that we think we are thinking. In many ways, this is
difficult to accept because we have convinced ourselves that our
thoughts have nothing to do with the things we see 'out there'.
Taking these ideas into account, we can understand what Jesus is
saying when he tells us how we are blindly leading each other
down an illusory path.

We are shown in this Saying as well as others how deeply we
sleep and flounder in a turbulent nightmare where we desperately search for a life line. The good news is that we can extricate
ourselves from this whirling vortex that is trying to pull us under
by grasping the extended hand of the Holy Spirit. As we see our
way clear, we extend that same helping hand to our brother so
that together we can celebrate our joyous reunion in the Truth.

Saying 40:
A grapevine has been planted outside of the Father, but since
it is not strong, it will be pulled up by its roots and shall pass
away.

The grapevine that Jesus is referring to is the illusory world of sin, disease and death and that is not of the Father. Our Father is the eternal, constant, unchanging Presence of Love. The world of turmoil could *not* be reality and stands outside of our Father's awareness. His Vision cannot include meaningless illusions for they are comprised of fabricated imaginings. Only the Vision of our immaculate Reality is held in His Pristine Gaze. Through the diligent practice of the principles of forgiveness, the illusory ego world with its erroneous concepts will eventually fade away and leave the perfection of the real world in its place.

It seems to be a contradiction when we speak of the world as being unreal, for it certainly seems that we are having a bodily experience. We must realize though, that the world's illusion of authenticity and its seeming power over our senses only results from our *belief* in its apparent reality which gives it legitimacy in our minds. We do not realize that we are immersed in a thought system that continues to limit our minds' perspectives so that we will never look beyond it to what is Real.

As we interpret everyday events with this familiar ego mindset, those thoughts create all of our outlooks and opinions. Conversely, if we decide to listen to the serene Voice of the Holy Spirit, our thoughts about reality will change. When those thoughts are altered our world view will also change. We will see things as they are, and this world for what it is because we will be relying on our Real Self. Let us remember that we are constantly choosing to give reality to either errors (illusions) or to Truth, and we can change our thought processes at a moment's notice.

Our present view of life is akin to a virtual reality game that gives the appearance of a garden or the streets of a city to a player, who then thinks that what is seen and heard is really happening, but all the while they are sitting at home in a chair. When we see the unequivocal truth of this world's unreality as it *really* is, then we will have stepped into the real world which is also our 'right mind'. As our minds change, we will indisputably know that we have always existed but just not as we had thought.

However, let us understand that Jesus is not advocating for us to ignore the suffering that takes place on this planet or the perspective of our bodies. What he *does* advocate is a *mind* conversion, a change as to which thought system we choose to embrace. With this new mindset we can climb out of the canyons of despair that we have inadvertently tumbled into.

As we adopt the Holy Spirit's way of thinking, we are firmly set upon the road to finding inner Peace. As we choose His thought system we will find that even if our environment or circumstances do not physically change, our mindset will be transformed and those same events will be interpreted with new eyes. When we have had a glimpse of our Father's Kingdom, the grapevine that was planted outside of our Father's House cannot sustain us nor do we want it to. We will clearly see the illusory nature of the world from a position outside of the dream. It is then that we have the Christic vision that sees the present world differently;

> Things which seem quite solid here are merely shadows there; transparent, faintly seen, at times forgot, and never able to obscure the light that shines beyond them. Holiness has been restored to vision, and the blind can see.[42]

This quote conveys the contrast between the dream and the real world where all illusions fade. It also revisits Saying 34, which speaks of blindness and the restoration of vision.

It bears repeating that when we speak of mind; we are not speaking about the body's human brain, but about the decision maker's mind that is outside of time and space that is making the choice as to how to see things in the world. This correlates as well to this Saying of the grapevine (world) being outside of the Father. The Son's Mind is where we, as the united One Son, made the original mistaken choice to side with the ego. This is the site where we need to return to so that we can start over and reverse our faulty decision.

Until now, we have blindly chosen the ego's thought system and believed that it advocated reality. The truth still remains that we have invested in nothingness, and that emptiness includes most importantly, the unreal thought of separation. It is unreal because in our unlimited Mind we have never left Heaven.

The Holy Spirit, Who is eternally in our Mind, gives us the opportunity at any time to choose what is true. Since our mind has never left our Source, we only need to perceive it as such to be returned. The full awareness of the Atonement, forgiveness and undoing of error is the recognition that *the separation never occurred.*[43] We have to move through a deeply imbedded resistance and fear to come to this point of recognition, so it may feel safer to advance at a slower, more tentative rate. To dwell in God's Love is our natural state and it *will* be fulfilled at the appointed time. This is His Will and cannot be denied. In the end we will find to our surprise that it was only our ego mind that had labeled this teaching of mind reversal as a difficult and arduous path.

As this Saying indicates, we shall perceive that the world is not strong and will pass away. It is not strong because it is based on only an illusion of strength and solidity. The Father's House is changelessly perfect and complete. As we shift our thinking to this mindset of the Holy Spirit, we realize as the One Son that we want only the permanence of the everlasting Kingdom, eternal life, and nothing else. As we accept the real world, we come to recognize that the things of the ego world are no longer desired, for they can never replace the eternal joy that is found in the Oneness of our Father's embrace and the sense of completeness in His thought system. It is only in this thought that we will find our true happiness. This is again referred to in the following Saying, where we are advised to disregard the world's temptations because of their lack of worth.

Saying 56:

Whoever has come to understand this world has found merely a corpse, and whoever has discovered the corpse, of that one the world is no longer worthy.

One who is no longer worthy of the world is one whose understanding has overcome the world, and now sees truly. Dreams of chaos, anarchy, and death have been replaced with the true vision of the real world that is timeless, changeless and forever unified. The Son looks upon all as his Father does and is consciously connected to the Light of the real world, seeing everything infused with joy and peace beyond comprehension. He understands the distress of the world but his peace is not affected by it, for he knows its unreality. He tenderly ministers to his brothers with love and devotion, and his Divine awareness is undeniably joined in Oneness to his brother's by the eternal Mind of the Father.

This Saying and the one following have at their core the same message to overcome our previous perceptions of the world. As we do, the world's emptiness becomes evident.

Saying 110:

J said, 'Let one who has found the world, and has become wealthy, renounce the world.'

As we make our way in the world and acquire understanding, we come to find that the world truly does not offer us anything of value. We realize that we have only been momentarily happy as we obtained some acknowledgement, praise or item. Even if we believed we were finally satisfied, that satisfaction soon lost its appeal, and we searched again, looking to the next occasion and the next transitory item to make us 'happy'. We have deluded ourselves by thinking that happiness can be attained by 'something out there', and thereby have unwittingly played the ego's game. And so our lives have revolved.

This is like the proverbial 'carrot on a stick' mentality, where we chase down our happiness as various desires present themselves, but the perceived happiness that we seek is always just out of reach, just beyond our grasp. This mindset keeps us running around in circles so that we will never look for alternatives.

As we mentally mature and realize this pattern, we recognize that we long for the permanence of something that has been beyond our awareness. We have begun to discover that happiness will not be found outside of ourselves in the objects or events of the world. We see that the dreams of those myriad distractions have kept us from discerning our real goal and function which is joining with the everlasting constancy of God.

Now we can set our sights on gaining the valuable, which is God's Kingdom, and renounce the valueless, which is the ego's world that has brought us nothing but mental anguish. This is the change that comes from within; this is the change that we seek. This is the only change that has lasting permanence, for it leads us to the joy and peace of God that is beyond all things transitory.

Saying 31:
    A prophet is not acceptable in his own town. A doctor does
    not heal those who know him.

We think we know someone from their actions, appearance, and profession or from our experiences with them in the past. What we actually have done is ascribed a judgment upon them based on our own assessments. As the *Course* is founded on the prospect of changing of our thinking, Jesus relays that we do not know our brother as the Holy Spirit knows him to be; as God's Son, perfect, holy and One. If we rely on our limited senses to make an assessment, the resulting judgment is unquestionably limited and inadequate. The Holy Spirit sees the complete picture of our Divine Reality, and therefore only He can judge for Truth.

As we become teachers and students of the Holy Spirit's precepts, we will find that those who knew us before we changed on inner levels will still see us as the same as before, for people cannot see beyond their own preconceived ideas and understanding.

Nevertheless, there are no accidents in salvation. If we view our brother as one with us, it is not necessary for him to comprehend our altered views. He may see that we have a more serene brow or loving smile, and that is enough. We do not need to pronounce our beliefs, wear certain talismans or perform specific rituals to prove our sincerity or devotion. What does occur on inner levels is that as we transform our thinking, the entire Sonship changes and moves forward. This happens as the teacher makes a single decision to view his brother differently. Therefore, to change the world it only takes one Son of God Who is aware of Who He is.

We attract those with whom an encounter is mutually essential, and that includes everyone who is within our sphere of influence. Now with our expanded awareness we can be certain that every incident that happens in our lives is an opportunity to see our brother differently and therefore becomes a Holy Encounter that can save the world.

Following are a few more interesting Sayings by Jesus for our consideration. We will explore their underlying meaning and correlate them with *a Course in Miracles*.

Saying 32: J said, 'A city built on a high hill and fortified cannot fall, nor can it be hidden.'

Saying 76: J said, 'God's Divine Rule is like a merchant who had a supply of merchandise and then found a pearl. That merchant was prudent; he sold the merchandise and bought the single pearl for himself. So also with you, seek the treasure that is unfailing, that is enduring, where no moth comes to eat and no worm destroys.'

Saying 63: There was a rich person who had a great deal of money. He said, 'I shall invest my money so that I may sow, reap, plant, and fill my storehouses with produce, that I may lack nothing.' These were the things he was thinking in his heart, but that very night he died.

Saying 96: J said, 'God's Divine Rule is like a woman. She took a little leaven, hid it in dough, and made it into large loaves of bread. Anyone here with two ears had better listen!'

When Saying 32 speaks about a 'city on a high hill', the Saying imparts that once we decipher who we are, and experience our inherent God Reality, we will shine as a beacon in the night from that lofty hill. Our awareness of the Divine will be resolutely established, and its radiance will not be hid. That luminous understanding will become a rallying call for our brothers to ascend the 'high hill' as well.

Saying 76 runs along similar lines. It speaks of consciously striving for the priceless 'pearl' as the enduring gift of our inheritance, the realization that we are unequivocally loved beyond our imagining. The merchant had been in the world but came upon the knowledge of his true essence, and has put all other pursuits behind him. His eye has become single, focused and unified, and his body is filled with light.[44] Once we have found this pearl of great price our path will become clear and our objective certain. We aspire to nothing else; because we realize that there *is* nothing else. The knowledge and love of the Divine is eternally ours and can never be taken away or destroyed, for it rests in timelessness.

On the other hand, Saying 63 demonstrates how we cannot save ourselves by trying to secure our safety in the material world. This world of our own making offers no shelter or sanctuary; it is a world of change and turmoil, and trying to hold onto any aspect of it will only offer disappointment and sorrow.

This Saying also reveals our fear of lack, and the competitive aspect of the ego mind that tries to satiate that lack at the expense of another. We believe in the falsehood of gaining security by buttressing the fortifications and possessions around our bodies. The mental and physical exertion required for this semblance of security is exhausting, and sidetracks us from changing our awareness to that of our true purpose. As we see the contrast between this world of chaos and the real world of light and peace that transcends all things transitory, we come to realize that our only safety lies in our union with God that offers us peace everlasting.

In Saying 96, God's Divine Rule is another way to say God's Laws. This Saying speaks symbolically of the Holy Spirit within, which we have as yet not given our attention to. As we grow in awareness and nurture that 'little bit of leaven', that spark of the Holy Spirit will grow and multiply. Once our focus is on what is real, that Love extends to enfold the world, and the knowledge of our Unity will extend and develop without limit.

We grow in our awareness of Spirit by sharing. If we stay in the ego mindset, immersed in our fear of lack, love cannot increase and will only stagnate. Without touching upon the 'leaven' of the Holy Spirit, we cannot break the bonds of our limited physical perceptions to emerge from the sludge of the world that seeks to pull us under.

It is important to note that Jesus repeatedly mentions having eyes to see and ears to hear. We therefore must not pass over these Sayings quickly, for he directs us to pay particular attention and look beyond the literal words to their fundamental spiritual meaning.

Saying 111:
  J said, 'The Heavens and the earth will roll up in your presence, and whoever is living with the living one will not

see death. Did not I say, 'Those who have found themselves, of them the world is not worthy'?'

The thought form most often repeated throughout *The Gospel of Thomas* is that we 'will not see death'. This phrase emphasizes the teaching of overcoming the world, letting us know our Reality is not of this world and death like all else, is an illusion of endings. To embrace the precepts of the Living One and change our thinking about the world and its reality is to follow a path that leads to eternal Life.

This Saying also repeats a portion of Saying 56, where 'of them the world is not worthy', and is another example of how these thoughts are interrelated. These Sayings continually reveal that the world is not worthy of us, for it is not our Home. Our Eternal Home resides in the bosom of our Creator where thoughts of death and dying are dismissed for the dream that they are. Jesus continually reminds us that we are made of the substance of Heaven and that the grandeur of our Being is categorically beyond anything that appears to manifest in this temporal world. It is only our attention that can be diverted to the trifling offerings that we are tempted with. When we shift our focus and become cognizant of our priceless treasure, our consciousness will rise above unreality and move into the awareness of our Divine estate.

Saying 113:
The disciples said to him, 'When will the Kingdom come?' He said, 'It will not come by watching for it. It will not be said, 'Behold here,' or 'behold there.' Rather, the Kingdom of the Father is spread out upon the earth and people do not see it.'

The disciples were grounded in a corporeal consciousness (as we are), looking for answers in a physical universe. Jesus was informing them that the Kingdom is not physical, in a specific place or even in the earth. It cannot be seen with the body's eyes because the Kingdom is in the Mind, and is unalterably in *our* minds, but we do not yet have the vision to see that it is so. Our vision becomes lucid as we join with Jesus and rise above the battlefield of chaos and confusion, [45] and recognize that we are not a body but as God created us, as eternal Spirit. This recognition heralds the end of our belief in the consciousness of sin, punishment and death.

Step by step, we come to the understanding that we walk with God in perfect holiness. In fact, Jesus tells us in the *Course;* 'You cannot walk the world apart from God, because you could not be without Him. He is what your life is.'[46] Further, 'Whatever you do you do in Him, because whatever you think, you think with His Mind.'[47] As we remember our Source, we can rest in the awareness of the Light of our Divine Reality. 'God has lit your mind Himself, and keeps your mind lit by His Light, because His Light is what your mind is.'[48]

These timeless Sayings which are mirrored in the canonical gospels, have endured throughout the ages because as Jesus, the supreme teacher of men, speaks to the disciples he is also speaking to us. He relays ageless teachings that help us navigate the twists and turns of our life's path.

This Saying illustrates an insightful message, and tells us that as long as we believe in a body consciousness we will not have true vision. The body's eyes were not made to look within to find the Kingdom, but made to perceive outwardly into the ego's world. Thus, when we gazed upon the world's attractions we would believe that they offered meaning and their actual meaninglessness would be obscured. Our physical eyes, and all that they look upon and judge, are a product of the ego thought system that would condemn us to never lift our spiritual eyes up toward our Heavenly Father. Let us look with the Holy Spirit's eyes to see beyond the trappings of this mortal world and see all with a new interpretation that will liberate our minds.

The following passage from the Text gives clarity to the concept of the divided mind that makes choices amongst illusions. As we mentioned previously, when we ask the ego what our purpose is, we are asking the question of the one in the entire universe that does not know. We cannot ask an illusion to explain itself and honestly expect a reliable answer. It is apparent that we need to step outside of the dream and ask the question of the One who can give us the only true Answer. The following excerpt explains this predicament that we find ourselves in.

> The world asks but one question. It is this: 'Of these illusions, which of them *is* true? Which ones establish peace and offer joy? And which can bring escape from all the pain of which this world is made?' Whatever form the question takes, its purpose is the same. It asks but to establish sin is real, and answers in the form of preference....And this is not a question, for it tells you what you want and where to go for it...An honest question is a learning tool that asks for something that you do not know. It does not set conditions for response, but merely asks what the response should be. But no one in a conflict state is free to ask this question, for he does not *want* an honest answer where the conflict ends.[49]

As we turn our attention to the Holy Spirit and take His hand, we are led ever forward toward our right mind. We will be able to ask for and receive an honest answer without being sidetracked by any of our interfering preconceived notions. In the past we had thought that we knew the answer before the question was asked, since we had already picked out the 'right' answer from amongst our images.

As we now put aside these preconceived thoughts, we will hear the quiet Answer from beyond the dream and will be able to embrace the happiness that ends all conflict. We will once again see Reality, and will marvel that it could ever have been obscured from our awareness. The Workbook defines true vision:

Christ's vision has one law. It does not look upon a body, and mistake it for the Son whom God created. It beholds a light beyond the body; an idea beyond what can be touched, a purity undimmed by errors, pitiful mistakes, and fearful thoughts of guilt from dreams of sin. It sees no separation. And it looks on everyone, on every circumstance, all happenings and all events, without the slightest fading of the light it sees…(as errors are) unseen by (the) One they merely disappear, because a vision of the holiness that lies beyond them comes to take their place.[50]

As we look at the Saying again and parallel it with the above excerpt, we can see how we have blocked the sight of the splendor that continually surrounds us. We have mistakenly sought for answers in the world of effects, where there are no answers. We add to our confusion by vainly trying to prove that we are 'right' that we chose the world as our teacher. The question is; do we want to be right or happy? [51]

The answer is that in the end we will never be satisfied with our ego constructs or choices because they have led us away from our true purpose. This is easily remedied by shifting our minds to our new Teacher Who knows the Answer that will gain us our everlasting happiness. This is pointed out in the following passage;

Many have chosen to renounce the world while still believing its reality. And they have suffered form a sense of loss, and have not been released accordingly. Others have chosen nothing but the world, and they have suffered from a sense of loss still deeper which they did not understand. Between these paths there is another road that leads away from loss of every kind…[52]

As we step back and let the Holy Spirit lead the way, He will go before us lighting a path for all to follow, and He will reveal the comforting Truth that we remain, and are as God created us.

In the following quote from A *Course in Miracles* the Kingdom is spoken about in a non-dualistic manner, as well as conveying a beautiful thought form:

Heaven is not a place nor a condition. It is merely an awareness of perfect Oneness, and the knowledge that there is nothing else; nothing outside this Oneness, and nothing else within.[53]

Indeed, these teachings come from outside of time bringing the light to a darkened world. To understand the thought form of Oneness, we must come to realize:

There is nothing outside you. That is what you must ultimately learn, for it is the realization that the Kingdom of Heaven is restored to you.[54]

We are saved when we realize there is nothing outside of the awareness of the perfect Oneness of God, and in that realization we reclaim our rightful legacy. It seems to be distant but is as close to us as our thoughts.

86. J said, 'Foxes have their dens and birds have their nests, but human beings have no place to lay down and rest.'

Even though this interesting Saying seems to be contra-dictory, it ties into the inherent message of all of the Sayings in *Thomas' Gospel*. We may question how the animals in nature will find rest and humans never shall.

Jesus brings to light why we will never find rest on the material plane, or in worldly pleasures. This world is not our place of origin. Man will not find peace until he decides to embark upon the spiritual journey back to his Father's House. The only place where we will find our true happiness and our long sought after peace is in our Father's Embrace.

We have vainly searched for serenity in this world and have only found disappointment. When we have experienced enough dead ends and finally throw up our hands and say, 'There must be a better way!' our eyes will cautiously open and we will notice a previously unseen path that has always been there beckoning us to follow. Here is the path where we will at long last find our joyful rest and heart's desire.

Saying 6:

The disciples asked him, 'Do you want us to fast? How should we pray? Should we give to charity? What diet should we observe?' J said, 'When you go into any region and walk in the countryside, and people take you in, eat what they serve you. After all, what goes into your mouth will not defile you; rather, it's what comes out of your mouth that will reveal you.'

Here again, the disciples demonstrate that they are in the worldly consciousness by asking worldly questions. They have not realized that behavior or anything that is done in this world does not affect the inherent majesty that resides in each and every one of us. It does not matter what or how we eat. It is not the behaviors that make or break us; what matters is what we think.

To remove the forgetfulness of our innate memory of God, we need to change our *thoughts* from those of hatred, attack and fear to thoughts of the inherent Love of our Father in every circumstance. Let us recognize that the thoughts of fear that we have made are not real, and as they are not real, they have not happened.

All fear is a part of the ego's illusory projection. Fear is the single emotion of the ego that is played out in numerous ways, always with the intent of keeping us separated from our Source and results in a lethal domino effect in our consciousness.

First there is anger over a perceived attack, (what our brother did, why or how could they have done this or that...) and to 'protect' our hurt feelings (the ego) we counter-attack, immediately feeling guilty because that attack is considered to be a 'sin' (we shouldn't have, we should be more forgiving...) and we consequently fear the punishment that our guilt claims that we merit for those 'sinful' thoughts or actions. We additionally envision God standing at the door waiting to mete out our much deserved punishment for these 'travesties'.

In panicked response, we subconsciously project that fear back out immediately. Then, as we see these 'unwarranted' attacks bouncing back to us that we had sent out in the first place, we start the whole cycle again. We have never realized that it is the ego's drama that we unconsciously keep perpetuating.

Actually, we do not need to examine and dredge up our fearful thoughts from their subterranean depths to have them vanquished. We only need to be aware that they are there and that they motivate our behaviors and actions. As we observe their deleterious effects, we now have the ability to make another choice, to think differently and embrace the Truth of our Divine Reality and then we can joyfully cast aside our unwanted preconceived judgments.

When errors in our thoughts crop up, let us not deny their existence, but ask for the strength of our Guide to be able to review them without condemnation, fear or denial. We are thus giving ourselves permission to follow them to their illogical conclusion. As we do so, we will come to recognize their unreality and lack of ability to take away our peace, and we will experience a positive sense of release. As we do this exercise consistently, layers of negativity will steadily fall away.

Our anchor in Truth is the knowledge that God cannot be diminished in any way. We have and always will abide with Him in the Eternal Now. We have only feared a nightmare of our own making which has not occurred.

To try to change one's behavior patterns by a force of the ego's will (in other words, trying to do it on our own without the Holy Spirit's help), does not work and the results are only temporary. If we try to force a physical change, we cannot succeed because we are trying to undertake a change in effects, where the problem is not, and consequently fall deeper into the world's dream.

A rule of thumb would be that anytime we feel guilty about our behavior or thoughts—we are in the ego's thought system. Our task becomes to look beyond the *effects* of this world. Those effects are the appearances that we perceive to be real and take so seriously. We now look to the Holy Spirit to guide us to take us beyond the body's perceptions. We will then recognize and depend on our true Strength because we are relying on His guidance.

Again, nothing you do or think or wish or make is necessary to establish your worth…You ego is never at stake because God did not create it. You spirit is never at stake because He did.[55]

To reiterate, in this Saying Jesus gently tells the disciples that it is not behavior (as in following strict guidelines of what to eat, or how to pray) in the world that is important, but what they think. Forgiving thoughts are displayed and are made manifest in the world through words and actions. When our purified thoughts reveal the light of the Holy Spirit's thought system of forgiveness in the world, our words and actions are naturally aligned with God's Will.

Thus, *the Light of those divine thoughts becomes perceptible actions in the world of form.* This is the Holy Spirit's thought system in action. When our deeds are in alignment with God's Will, they will be seen and integrated by our brother who is an extension of our One Self, and we are both saved. As our minds become unified through this process, the keystone of the bridge to eternity is set in place, and we tread lightly across its sturdy foundation to embrace all that is Real.

Saying 24:
> The disciples said, 'Show us the place where you are, for we must seek it.' He said to them, 'Anyone here with two ears had better listen! There is light within a person of light, and it shines on the whole world. If it does not shine, it is dark.'

The disciples saw the Light surrounding Jesus, inspiring them to seek the Light for themselves. This is as it should be. When *we* come to embrace the nature of our True Identity, our brother will be drawn to the light that is ever present within us, and as he is drawn to us, he will see the selfsame light within himself. He will recognize our guiltlessness as well as his own, and he will understand that he is as beloved of his Father as we are.

The next section of this Saying may seem to be an obvious statement, where 'if it does not shine, it is dark', but there is more to this expression than meets the eye. If we take into account our previous discussions about light and darkness, Spirit and the ego's world, then we know if we accept any part of the ego's world of darkness we become lost in that illusion ourselves. The Text of the *Course* underscores this important point by saying; 'Confusion is not limited. If it occurs at all it will be total.'[56] If we think attack in any form is justified, that faulty perception will block our knowledge of the Divine, and we will stay in darkness until that thinking is reversed.

To counteract our misguided allegiance to the wrong thought system we have to recognize our brother's needs as our own. His call for love is ours, his negatives and positives are reflections of our own. Consequently, as his very presence mirrors every aspect of ourselves back to us, he is continually creating forgiveness opportunities for us.

Now as we come to identify an offending aspect of our brother, we make the conscious effort to transcend our previous judgments and prejudices. As we endeavor to exchange our ego thoughts for those of the Living One, we are healing our sense of fragmentation and separation. Since we have begun to understand that what is the same is seen as One, we are beginning the process of melding our ideas of separation into Wholeness.

To prevent the psychological frustration that occurs when we catch ourselves being critical or judgmental of anything, we must realize that everyone's *first* thought in *any* situation is that of judgment. When we understand this, we calmly and quickly switch to the Holy Spirit's thought system that assures us of the meaninglessness of the egos thoughts. Let us keep in mind that even as we are immersed in the process of learning the ways of the Holy Spirit, we will find ourselves alternating back and forth between thought systems. It is comforting to know that as we advance in our thinking processes that we will find ourselves holding the Holy Spirit's hand more consistently and for longer periods of time, and then the joyous moment will come when that handfast becomes permanent.

As we participate in the amphitheater of life we are aware of how people come together in relationships, jobs, sports or other playing fields. We see that all events are permeated in competition, always opposing another person, group or nation. Our aspiration is to change our minds about the long held concepts that we have had about rivalry in the world.

Let us strive to embrace the thought that our only common interest is to be One in our awareness with our brother. Not to view him as enemy or competitor, or as one who has more or less than us, but to see ourselves as one united consciousness that transcends separate interests. When that consciousness is achieved, our light will shine out from the darkness and light the whole world.

As we move forward in our quest for Unity, we are reminded

many times in the Text by Jesus to pay attention to our thoughts as we move throughout the day. To keep our purpose clear and in the forefront of our minds, we should be 'vigilant *against* this idea (of competition), because all your conflicts come from it...and (you) have accepted the impossible as true.'[57] And what is the impossible? To believe that conflicting interests are possible, and believe that they have been achieved.

We have been at odds with the idea that God's equal Sons have everything, no more or less than the other. Know that only equals can be at Peace. When we have the sure knowledge of the Everything and the Everywhere, there is no need or desire for competition.

Saying 37:

> When you take your clothes off without guilt, and you put them under your feet like little children and trample them, then you will see the son of the living one and you will not be afraid.

Our eyes will open with delight as we surmount the fabricated guilt of our thoughts of separation. We cast off the chains (clothes) that had bound our thoughts with illusions, and we now bask in the joy of our freedom from limitations!

In this Saying, Jesus is not speaking of the guilt or shame of the body consciousness but about the guilt of the separation thought that is deeply embedded in the Mind of the Son. Now, since we have chosen to change our mind and accept the eternal Laws of God that never vary and in which there is no loss of any kind, we will transcend the worlds' limiting parameters.

The immutable, unchanging and ever-present Love of God is our heritage. When we have accepted the endless joy that our Father offers us, we will transcend and trample underfoot this world's consciousness. We will boldly walk forward and tread fearlessly through the guilt that never was, leaving behind all fear and judgment. We will see the Light that is within all and recognize our brother as he is.

26. You see the speck that is in your brother's eye, but you do not see the log that is in your own eye. When you take the log out of your own eye, then you will see clearly enough to take the speck out of your brother's eye.

36. Do not worry, from morning to night and from night until morning, about what you will wear.

54. Fortunate are the poor, for yours is the Father's Kingdom.

The 'log in our own eye' in Saying 26, is referring to our being blinded by our criticism and judgment of others. Our vision becomes so clouded that all that is seen is our brothers provoking affront. This envisioned offense, which is nothing in comparison with our own blindness, fills our consciousness so completely that it throws us directly into the ego's thought system of anger and criticism. We have made the ego's world real and can no longer see anything else. It is truly a part of the great projection that seeks to lay blame on others, and not take responsibility for our own thoughts.

This provocation, which in actuality is nothing more than a mere 'speck' of an erroneous thought, can be disregarded with the help of the Holy Spirit. We can now choose to see the unreality of the error and the innocence of God's Son beyond the form. Only then can we see past the seeming offense, and illusions are seen as illusions, not as Truth. Our blindness to our unity is now revealed, and the error dissolves before our eyes. The 'log' of unforgiveness comes out of our eye, and the nothingness of the 'speck' in our brother's eye disperses.

As we let go of attack and malice against our brother, our own blindness dissolves and we see the same innocence in him that our Father sees in His One Son. The speck is just a dust mote that blows away in the wind, and it is then that we recognize our Self.

As we humbly ask the Holy Spirit for the gentle guidance to come to this awareness of true vision that is beyond the form of the error, we know with calm assurance that as we have asked, so we have received.

In Sayings 36 and 54 we find that Jesus is speaking metaphorically, and not referring to how we should conduct ourselves in the world. He tells us not to be mentally attached to the results of our endeavors in this world by placing undue value on worldly possessions. To expand on this thought, another word for 'poor' mentioned in Saying 54 could be 'unattached', where we are unconcerned about physical outcomes because our thoughts have been transformed to the Reality of the Holy Spirit's thought system.

Some may take these two Sayings to literally mean not to worry about anything in the physical realm, and then feel guilty if the desire to have belongings, assets or wealth arises. We must realize that there is nothing wrong with possessions in and of themselves as we need certain things in this world for our physical survival. The only important thing is how we view those possessions. If they become an end in and of themselves, then we are in the ego's framework.

On the other hand, we would be in our right mind if we remain unattached to material things and recognize that their only function is to maintain our bodies so that we can move forward spiritually. A good policy to follow is to ask ourselves whose hand we are holding as we go about our day. These Sayings impart to us is to be mindful of who our Teacher is and as we are, we will find that this is what will determine what we place our value upon.

The world may seem substantial and real, but so do the images in our sleeping dreams while we slumber. When we wake those dreams evaporate into nothingness, so too our waking dreams when we waken to the Truth as to who we are beyond the dream. We see the dream for what it is with Jesus, from a vantage point outside of time. As he helps us to mentally disengage from the ego's thought system, we become more aware of our real Self, which brings us one step closer to our innate memory of God.

The aforementioned mindset of non-attachment is also true of the next Saying that is short and to the point.

42. Be passersby.

This again refers to being mentally detached from worldly concepts and objects. It suggests to emotionally detach from our past judgments and prejudices which have only served to tether us to the wrong mind.

As we let these thoughts go into the Light of God's gentle awareness, knowing we would rather be 'happy' with the Holy Spirit's assessments, than 'right' about the ego's judgments[58] we find forgiveness and love flood our being with happiness and joy and we are unburdened from our self-imposed fetters. With this vision we can easily 'pass by' the temptations that would seek to bind our minds, for we have had a glimpse of the eternal.

Saying 100:
> They showed J a gold coin and said to him, 'The Roman Emperor's people demand taxes from us.' He said to them, 'Give the Emperor what belongs to the Emperor. Give God what belongs to God.'

This Saying, also found in the New Testament, brings up an interesting point. Jesus was not really speaking of money, but stating this: 'Let Caesar have the things of this world, for they are nothing. Let God have your spirit, for it is everything.'[59] In other words, we need to leave the illusions of this world to 'Caesar' and strive to merge with the Truth that is beyond this earthly plane. Once again, Jesus speaks of changing one's mind as to what we consider important.

This Saying is also in alignment with several other Sayings that focus on merging with the Truth of our One Mind, and the importance of setting our sights upon our one true goal and not be distracted by falsehoods. Some examples would include Saying 47 which states that 'we cannot serve two masters', God and materiality. It instructs us to put our priorities in order and focus on attaining the awareness of the Kingdom versus getting lost in the ego construct. Another example is Saying 36, which tells us not to 'worry from morning till night about what we will wear'. That would lead to our being focused on external things rather than being attentive to the goal of attaining our true treasure within.

The inherent message of these Sayings concentrates on expanding our inner awareness so that we can come to know who we really are beyond form. Instead of concentrating on outer accoutrements, we are now focusing on the Eternal Spirit that resides within. That is our Everything, our life and our purpose, and there is nothing else.

As we ponder the composition and unity of these thoughtful Sayings and apply their precepts to our lives, they assist us in remembering our goal of realigning our thoughts with Spirit.

95. If you have money, do not lend it at interest. Rather, give it to someone who will not pay you back.

We understand this Saying to indicate the process of detachment from materiality as well. It also demonstrates the ultimate unimportance of the material things of this dream world. If we lose our peace over 'what is owed', we then know we have identified with thoughts of scarcity and lack, and have focused on the fearful world of loss and change. As we view the world with the Holy Spirit's eyes, He assures us that in God there is no lack and therefore as His Son we can lack nothing. We are reminded once again that all that we have done is chased after an insubstantial dream.

Let us remember that when we are speaking of 'needs' and 'lack', we are using the *Course's* definition of these terms. In other words, our sense of lack stems from the worldly view of constant conflict and competition in which the need to 'get' and to protect what we have 'gotten' is paramount. These ideas have not served us and have only bound us to illusions. We are becoming more aware of God's Eternal Love, that sees His Son as One with Him, and knows that His Son already has Everything. Now our objective is to walk consistently with Him Who judges not, and keep our attention focused upon right-minded thinking instead of falling into past traps of criticism, condemnation and judgment.

The circumstances in our lives are going to play out as they will; therefore what becomes important is the mindset in which we view those occurrences as they transpire. We need to be aware of our judgments that label events as 'good' or 'bad', or having 'abundance' or 'lack', for those labels are ego constructs that have been made to play a part in its bleak world. The right-minded view of *everything* that happens in the world is seen as our opportunity to forgive and embrace the Holy Spirit's thought system without labeling things with our preconceived judgments. What is ultimately important is to step back from the distracting events of our world and objectively witness their dream-like unreality. We can still partake in events but will not be lured into giving them a significance that they do not have.

The Law of Attraction
As we consider the import of our thoughts, an interesting concept to think about is the 'New Age' idea of the 'law of attraction'. This premise states that our positive or negative thoughts correspondingly attract all of the positive or negative circumstances into our lives. Obviously, there is nothing wrong with a positive interpre-

tation to our thoughts, for the grandeur of our Father's Kingdom is revealed through the beautiful symbols in this world, such as the love within a family, or a serene garden path... These heartfelt symbols help us see beyond the fear and guilt that subconsciously weigh us down and occlude our thoughts.

Let us only be mindful that we do not trick ourselves into thinking that we are optimistic and upbeat when we are actually 'pasting' a positive veneer over judgmental cynicism, and denying what we believe we are *really* seeing. If this happens, our thoughts are not in alignment with our interpretation of events and we will experience a subtle sense of unease, and will not understand the cause.

We recognize that every single perception that we have of the world radiates outward from our ego-minds, which is the seat of our judgments. As those judgments radiate out, they instantaneously come back to us, enacting a perpetual cosmic dance of give and take. This is the acting out of the law of attraction. We understand that if dissension flows out, this *error* will keep coming back, and we will view events from that skewed perspective until we change what we are sending out. We need not fret, but calmly change our negative interpretations, (by seeing from the Holy Spirit's perspective) and then our world view will change with it. This phenomenon is not either 'good' or 'bad', it is just a metaphysical law that we can change to our benefit as we become more aware. If we make a mistake, we need but to correct our view of it, not condemn ourselves for making that mistake or behaviorally try to change it.

Our objective is not to deny that we have negative thoughts, but only try to be aware of them as they inevitably crop up. Let us accept the fact that negative judgments will come about as we go about our day. If our thoughts are not in accord with the Holy Spirit's directives, we just give them over to Him and ask that we see all events as He does. We must not condemn ourselves for our judgmental thoughts or be fearful of any negative consequences to those thoughts, but gently realize that they are just errors and a product of past momentums. As we become mindful of these heretofore unrecognized judgmental thoughts and hand them over to the Holy Spirit, we will grow in the awareness of our True Nature.

A misinterpretation of this law plays out in the following manner. Let us consider how a person can become fearful when negative thoughts of the future arise, for example, potential sickness, bodily harm to oneself or loved ones, financial problems... If a person thought that consequences would materialize in their lives by thinking those fearful thoughts, then they would immediately try to dispel and 'neutralize' them (or deny their existence). Also, it could be very distressing that those thoughts appeared in the first place, letting even more unconscious guilt seep into the mind.

What we must ultimately realize is that we need not fear 'repercussions' because of thoughts that we may have had. As we objectively look at the law of attraction and observe those thoughts of fear (which are errors in thought), we will dismiss them as powerless to affect our lives. Then we will be using this law in alignment with the Holy Spirit.

We are now aware that any mode of thought that produces fear of reprisals in any capacity is not in accord with the Holy Spirit's principles. As a matter of fact, *to believe that thoughts produce consequences in the world is a concept that gives reality to the dream.*

As we examine these ideas together with the precepts of *A Course in Miracles,* we can use this law to move forward on our spiritual path. We recognize that the Holy Spirit's thought system will never bring about fear of any kind. He sees only the Truth of our Reality and dismisses the irrelevant errors of the dream. By the Grace of the Holy Spirit's Vision, we will also see beyond the limiting and binding confines of the ego world.

All fearful thoughts and ideas are a part of the egos thought system and have no power as they merely consist of vaporous daydreams. The only power that they have is the measure of our belief in them. Instead of ignoring or succumbing to our fears, subtle or otherwise, our objective is to have the awareness (vigilance) to bring those illusions to the Holy Spirit's attention so that we can once more step over the threshold of our Father's House and take up our rightful residence.

We easily forget that this world is not our real Home and that we are not actually 'living' here or having real experiences here. We are but dreaming of events and circumstances to forestall integration with our true Reality. At this point however, even as we may not be ready yet to fully accept the Holy Spirit's precepts, we can rest in the knowledge that our freedom is God's Will and it shall most assuredly come without struggle or strife at the preordained time in our lives.

We understand that the ego has many schemes, and its purpose is to keep us bound us to the world's ideas. If we remember that anything other than Love is a part of this illusory world then all fearful ideas are exposed as ego based. Ego based thoughts are a detour that diverts our attention from our true path. Consequently, if we get caught in the egos snare of fear, we will not recognize the Holy Spirit's true use of the mind that thinks *only* the loving thoughts of our Father, or realize that any thoughts other than Love are a part of the illusion. Our fears and all that they entail, need to be bravely looked at as part of the dream of separation, even as we simultaneously play our part in the world.

To recognize that these fears are miscreations of the ego mind and do not exist, is 'a far better protective device...because it introduces correction at the level of the error...and that correction belongs at the thought level.'[60] When we correct our thoughts, our mistaken ideas will evaporate and leave us in our Father's safe embrace.

As we come to rest in the safety of God and our fears drop

away, we realize we neither need nor want anything else but the continuous ever-present Peace and Love of our Father. To underscore this point, we are asked an earnest question by Jesus in *A Course in Miracles*:

'What way could give you more than everything, or offer less and still content the holy Son of God?'[61]

This is a poignant question, which we have not acknowledged as yet, because we still dwell in the dream of the ego world's reality. We have not realized as yet that we will not find contentment until we acknowledge our Eternal Self that is created by God and which is beyond all form. It is only then that we will see the world through His forgiving eyes and accept our Everything.

Here are a few more Sayings from *Thomas' Gospel* that are indicative of the Holy Spirit's thought system.

11. The dead are not alive, and the living will not die.

22. When you make the two into one, and when you make the inner like the outer and the outer like the inner, and the upper like the lower, and when you make male and female into a single one, so the male will not be male and the female will not be female...then you will enter the Kingdom.

49. Fortunate are those who are alone and chosen, for you will find the Kingdom. For you have come from it, and you will return there again.

In Saying 11, Jesus is speaking of the awakened resurrected mind, without which we are not truly living. He goes on to say that those whose minds have been enlightened will never die for in their awareness of Truth they have transcended the world. This is also indicative of the hidden meaning of the oft quoted line; 'will not taste death'.

In the Workbook Lesson headed 'I am as God created me'[62],

Jesus gives us an added insight on the meaning of Saying 11. It is as if 2000 years has been rolled up as a scroll and we sit again at the feet of the Master.

He begins by explaining the Workbook Lesson's heading 'I am as God created me' to be a sacred thought form. Our salvation lies within these words as we truly embrace them as our own, for they dispel dreams of sin and illusions of death. They speak God's Word to us, and tell of our Father's Love and our completion in Him, realigning our mind to think with His Holiness.

As he further elaborates upon the expression 'I am as God created me', he gives us a vision of awakening to the inner meaning of these words. They are heard as '...the trumpet of awakening that sounds around the world. The dead awake in answer to its call. And those who live and hear this sound will never look on death.'[63] As our brothers' hear the call of awakening, we all rise to greet our Father and realize our joyous unity and eternal bond.

When Saying 49 speaks of those who are alone and chosen, it speaks of those who know there *is* only One, and therefore their awareness has come full circle back to the beginning. When we choose to listen to the Living One we also become God's chosen ones. To regain our forgotten awareness, the path embarked upon requires diligence and constancy of purpose.

The curriculum of *A Course in Miracles* is a vehicle we can use to reignite our memory. Jesus will help us retrace our steps back to the beginning where we made the original decision to be separate from God. This is shown to us without condemnation, but with a gentle reminder of the error of our choice and the glad tidings that we can choose again.

Earlier we briefly discussed Saying 22, how it is consistent with the teachings of Jesus throughout these Sayings, as it reflects our unity as One Spirit beyond all perception of male or female form. It embraces the fullness of our Divine Reality as the

One Son in God's Mind, and it is where all thoughts of separation are healed.

The following Saying demonstrates how the disciples seek to put Jesus in a mundane worldly role and keep him to the letter of the law. It reveals how they blindly resisted listening to *his* immortal message which could have taken them beyond this dimension.

Saying 52:

The disciples said to him, 'Twenty-four prophets have spoken in Israel, and they all spoke of you.' He said to them, 'You have disregarded the living one who is in your presence, and have spoken of the dead.'

The disciples were still influenced by worldly praise, and were possibly thinking that Jesus would be complemented by the recognition of the prophets. Jesus admonished the disciples for listening to the worldly perceptions of the prophets that were steeped in the rigid, unyielding letter of the law. Their concepts were significantly different from his teaching. He chastised the disciples for ignoring the message of the Living Light Who is presently in their midst, and for only hearing messages from the ego's world that seeks to keep them entangled therein.

Jesus appeals to us as well to listen to the still small Voice that speaks the message of Oneness of the Holy Spirit, and not be deceived by the siren's call of the ego that is legion. The following Saying shows us how necessary the Holy Spirit is in bridging the gap.

Saying 66:

J said, 'Show me the stone that the builders rejected. That is the keystone.'

The keystone is instrumental in holding the arch together; both sides of the bridge rest upon it. Without the keystone the arch would collapse. The Holy Spirit is the keystone, and without His help we would lose sight of our goal and get caught on this side of materiality. He is the One to take us across the bridge that lies between this world and our Father's Kingdom. Conversely, the fabricated concepts that make up the world have been made by the builders who have rejected (turned away from) the Holy Spirit. We can see that the world has had the genuine 'key' of salvation in their midst but have dismissed it.

The Light will patiently wait and quietly support us even if it is unacknowledged and is presently rejected. When we are ready, the Living One gently leads us step by step across the bridge. As we choose His thought system of non-judgment we lay the foundation stone that makes our structure sturdy and our path secure.

Saying 89:

J said, 'Why do you wash the outside of the cup? Don't you understand that the one who made the inside is also the one who made the outside?'

This beautiful Saying relays an aspect of the majesty and completeness of God, wherein He is revealed everywhere and in everything. When we have eyes to see the beautiful symbols throughout the world that reflect God's abundant Love, we will experience the Peace that comes with that vision.

Adi Shankara (686-718 A.D.)[64] paralleled this lovely all-inclusive thought as he spoke of Brahman, God as the indivisible Oneness that Is; 'I am Brahman, the supreme, all-pervading like the ether, stainless, indivisible, unbounded, unmoved, unchanging. I have neither inside nor outside. I alone am. I am one without a second. What else is there to be known?'

We are as our Father Is, the One Son, created by the eternal Potter that *made* and *is* the cup and without Whom nothing that was made was made.

This excerpt and the Saying illustrate the all encompassing nature of God, and gives us a glimpse of our eternal, divine composition. It is truly a comfort to turn to our Real Self and find Peace in His enfolding Embrace.

Saying 18:

The followers said to J, 'Tell us how our end will be.' He said, 'Have you discovered the beginning, then, so that you are seeking the end? For where the beginning is, the end will be. Fortunate is the one who stands at the beginning: That one will know the end and will not taste death.'

The followers were asking Jesus about their 'end' in the world of form. Jesus kindly corrects them, saying we need to retrace our steps, going full circle back to the beginning to our awareness as Spirit. To do so, we need to relearn how to listen for the Voice for God by rising above the chattering ego mind. As we spend time every day with the Holy Spirit, we will teach ourselves to calmly listen in the silence for His guidance. As we do so, we will become aware of our true Self beyond the perception of form, and as a result our minds will be resurrected to rise above the worldly consciousness that will 'not taste death'.

There will be a time, promised to us by God, when we will return to the beginning before our dualistic nature took hold, and where we will find that the veils that had obscured our awareness have been lifted. There comes a time where the tangled ball of yarn of our confusion will rewind back into itself to disappear, and the ego and its machinations will be undone. We will hear only the Voice of the Living One, and the ego and its influence will have receded as our power of belief in it is withdrawn. At that time, in the text of A Course in Miracles, Jesus states: 'Where learning ends there God begins, for learning ends before Him Who is complete where He begins, and where there is no end.'[65]

This excerpt underscores the thought that once we have come full circle and unlearned and unraveled all of the impediments we have woven about ourselves, 'we will stand at the beginning', at One with our Father in His limitlessness without beginning or end. Thus we find this world melts away in the dawning knowledge that God's eternal Son 'will not taste death.'

One thing that we need to be aware of is that even though much has been 'seen' since our Beginning, nothing has really happened. The reason that we still become fearful (even though our True Self still resides in Peace) is because we have not yet gone back far enough to the starting point of Truth. As we approach the Beginning once more, we feel the fear of the destruction of the ego's thought system upon us as if it were imminent death. There is no death even though we have a belief that there is, and all beliefs are real to the believer until the Truth sets him free. [65A] We will look at this aspect of the dream in greater detail in an upcoming section.

We are unburdened from a very real sense of abandonment as we find ourselves standing together in timelessness with Jesus. We are reassured in *A Course in Miracles* of our inherent Oneness:

> To be alone is to be separated from infinity, but how can this be if infinity has no end?...There are no beginnings and no endings in God, Whose universe is Himself...Do you really believe that part of God can be missing or lost to Him?[66]

As we come to the awareness of the end at the beginning, it will become apparent that time has collapsed and the world and its illusions haven't *really* transpired, for in the limitlessness of God beginnings and endings are dreams. It is in this knowledge that we will know we are One.

Chapter Three

Three Enigmatic Parables

As we review these remarkable Sayings, a very interesting revelation comes to light regarding an undisclosed teaching from Jesus. Since Pursah recollects the life of Thomas the disciple, she revealed the undisclosed Sayings that Jesus spoke to Thomas the day that Jesus asked the disciples, to 'compare me to something and tell me what I'm like.'[1] Let us now take a look at these Sayings.

Continuation of Saying 13:

'And he took him, and withdrew, and spoke three sayings to him. When Thomas came back to his friends, they asked him, 'What did J say to you?' Thomas said to them, 'If I tell you one of the sayings he spoke to me, you will pick up rocks and stone me, and fire will come from the rocks and consume you.'

There has been a great deal of speculation as to what was said to Thomas at that time. Pursah said the reason Thomas did not reveal the three parables to the others is because Jesus had asked him not to, so that Thomas would be protected from accusations of blasphemy. The consciousness of the people of the time would not have comprehended the inner meaning of the Sayings, misconstruing the message and becoming fearful.

In this era, we who have eyes to see and ears to hear are blessed to receive these extraordinary insights. These are the three parables he said to Thomas:

You dream of a desert, where mirages are your rulers and tormentors, yet these images come from you.

Father did not make the desert, and your home is still with Him.

To return, forgive your brother, for only then do you forgive yourself.[1A]

We will examine these heretofore concealed Sayings to further develop the underlying message of the revised version of *The Gospel of Thomas* and parallel them with the teachings from *A Course in Miracles*.

These three previously undisclosed parables are quite significant, for they summarize the *Course's* teachings very succinctly, outlining the dream, its foundation and how we can overcome our illusions.

As our Source is God, and we realize He / Us are One, logically an idea of division cannot exist. A thought or dream of separation could *only* take place in a dream-like state that we have made up, and one that our Father is not aware of. Therefore the 'images' that we see could only come from us, for we are the ones who dream of separation and duality. We are the Dreamer of the dream, and the responsibility for the dream lies with us, even though we try to abrogate it. This is an important premise for it relays the idea that we are not subject to forces outside of our control, that rule and torment us, but rather *we* (as the One Son outside of time and space) make up these illusory perceptions and then choose to react to them. Such is the power of our Mind.

Fortunately for us, our safety and 'our home' have always rested in the all-encompassing Oneness of the Creator. We are forever supported in Love as our Reality, no matter the tiny illusions of a dreaming ego mind. These thoughts of a seeming separation and a separate world parallel the second Saying, 'Father did not make the desert, and our home is still with Him.'

As the third parable says, the only way to return to our God estate is to forgive our brother. As we do so, increment by increment, we find that what we were seeing in our brother was actually a reflection of our own thought processes, even though we did not recognize it as such. We can see that these parables are in alignment with all of our discussions so far.

To paraphrase a significant passage from a pamphlet that evolved from *A Course in Miracles*[2], we are given a simple formula as to how we can let go of the unforgiveness that clouds our perceptions. We recognize that only forgiveness can heal our mental and physical conditions, and it is unforgiveness, a synonym for judgment, that gave rise to the sickness in the first place. All we need do is realize that when we judge, criticize, or condemn our brother for *anything*, what we are really doing is casting disparagement onto the screen of his form for all that we have not forgiven in ourselves.

When we realize that this is what we have done, we have another opportunity to look at these judgments and re-evaluate them (certainly not condemn ourselves for having them). Then we will make the choice to hold the Holy Spirit's hand and let him help us forgive ourselves and our brother.

To let these momentums go successfully, we give ourselves permission to follow the negative ego thoughts through to their conclusion, and not deny that they have existed in our mind. We will then see how the ego's impact diminishes. Now we can confidently conclude that those unreal thought-forms have never affected our inherent Divinity at all.

This process lifts the burden of guilt (guilt over our attack thoughts, guilt of pride, judgment, separateness, fear, etc...) from our shoulders by allowing us to see beyond the form and its effects to look at the content. The content that we cling to is our unalterable Divinity and the realization that we are not separate but One.

This is how we look within. We now see that the unforgiving and judgmental thoughts that were projected out can be used for our review so that we can make another choice. This is how we recognize the dream that we have embroiled ourselves in, and we incrementally recognize that nothing has happened. This allows us to forgive ourselves *and* our brother for our misperceptions.

The first *thought* that starts us on our path Home is to realize that we want something beyond what this world has to offer. Thereafter, we begin to see that there is nothing that we have done in the world that impinges on the legacy of who we are in Reality.

We have given validity to the idea of terror in the past, but the *thought* that will set us free is that this idea of fear is *not* the substance from which we are made, and we are not part of its world. It is only an illusion in which dream figures battle, and where each figure upholds their own unreal dream of legitimacy.

When we hear the message of love and forgiveness that the *Course* imparts, we know that this is what we desire. We want the experience of our Creator as being One with us, and we also know that it is not the case presently. We must be careful to not think that we have lost our chance to become One with the ineffable Light because of actions that we have or have not done. This is a particularly virulent ego ploy that reinforces guilt and a sense of unworthiness. Our only task in this world is to erase the *thought* of guilt, for *that* is the cause of our sense of separation and has *nothing* to do with behavior.

To aid us in resolving this sense of separation, we must come to view time as a vast illusion in which even now our plan of salvation is woven in. The experience of God's revelation is already fixed for our life stream. Even if time and events appear to be random, the time of revelation does not alter, and we are assured that it will come at the appropriate time to every mind.

All events that seem to happen in time are already over and we are now resting in our Father's embrace. We only appear to be journeying along an arbitrary road that is perceived linearly. As we adopt this mindset we can let events unfold as they will and we will have a sense of peace as they do so.

As we experience ourselves dwelling in time now, every event that transpires in our lives gives us an opportunity to use time for a different purpose. As any negative judgment comes up, we can steadfastly replace it with Christ's vision that knows our brother's fundamental innocence and sees past the separation. This advanced view of forgiveness propels us forward toward accepting the real world instead of the ego's maladaptive one.

Also, to understand that all events happen in their own time sequence helps us to forgive the seeming 'slowness' of the process and we realize that it is only a subtle ego trick that would vie to push us to give up in impatient exasperation. As these unfolding forgiveness opportunities transpire, their function is to allow us to deal with them in peace, and let God be as He Is.

As we step back from our concept of the 'tormenting mirages', a terror filled world is seen for what it is; a fearful figment of the One Son's imagination run wild. We have made up this dream of confusion, fragmenting and projecting images out, and have forgotten *why*.

As we delve deeper and rediscover the reasons why we have made up these illusory obstacles to our True Vision, the real world opens up and we see that we *are* outside of the dream, looking *into* an illusory world. It is then we truly can see through 'eyes that forgiveness blesses' and we recognize that we 'are still with the Father'.

The real world is the happy outcome of seeing through forgiving eyes, and contains a 'sure correction for the sights of fear and sounds of battle which your world contains... (We will find) Only happy sights and sounds can reach the mind that has forgiven itself... (and) the world it sees arises from a mind at peace with itself.'[3] We see the same events that others do, but our interpretation has changed, and we see them for the illusions that they are. This is the last dream before we wake completely and go unto our Father.

Illusions are illusions and are false. Your preference gives them no reality. Not one is true in any way and all must yield with equal ease to what God gave as answer to them all. God's Will is One.[4]

Chapter Four

The Body's Function

Now that we are aware of the ego's tactics and understand that we have been engulfed by insane thinking that is the complete antithesis of Reality, we can implement all of the aforementioned 'tools' and climb rung by rung out of the pit of despair and heartache.

As we have discussed, up to this point we have accepted the mindset of the ego and its dream of forgetfulness, and it seemed that we were victims of circumstance. Again, we are speaking of the Mind of the One Son that believes that he has separated from his Source and is having a dream of fragmentation, not specific individuals. The One Son first believed in these concepts, fragmented and *then* those choices led to our varied problems and were made manifest in the world.

We have come to understand that the second, or world's dream was fabricated to keep the thought of separation from our Source solidly in place. The manifestation of this ego tactic is the belief in, and the identification with the body. The body is an instrument of the ego that only allows into its field of vision those things that testify to its reality and solidity, therefore keeping the illusion firmly in place.[1] The body becomes the focus of all of our attention and concern, keeping us distracted from awakening to seek our inherent purpose of reunion with our Father, and that we are not alone.

What we have not realized is that we will never be satisfied with anything less than the eternal. Since the body came into existence by an ego thought that is never content, we can conclude that the body as a product of that thought system could never be satisfied either. The body is an invention of the ego thought system, *and the body's intrinsic dissatisfaction has never left its source.*

Remember, the reason for the creation of the universe *and* the body was the Son's guilt over the separation, and he subsequently hid in a world of his own making to escape God's vengeance. The body consciousness is one of the last and most solid fortifications that was built as the last line of defense.

This deep-seated guilt over the separation produced the illusory, but seemingly very real fear of the repercussions to look within and to see ourselves beyond form as Spirit. This is the predicament that we find ourselves in now but are striving to overcome. Now as we change our allegiance to the Teacher Who will always guide us to the right Answer; we will be gently told that we have only made an easily correctable mistake.

If we view the world with the ego's eyes; we will see perpetual attack, defense and fear. As long as we align ourselves with this projection, we ensure the ego's survival and will be ensnared in its web of duplicity that continually perpetuates the dream of a world with its attendant problems.

This error addresses Thomas' concealed parable that speaks of the 'desert that is not of the Father' where 'mirages and tormentors reign', and also informs us that those 'images come from us.' Images and specters rise and fall to the tune that we have orchestrated, and only we can extricate ourselves from their cruel nightmare. Our perspective has become distorted; where our divine nature seems like the dream, a distant echo of a Reality forgotten, and the mirage has risen to take Reality's rightful place.

The Workbook speaks in depth about the body and its function. It behooves us to look at this aspect of the body so that we can be aware of its part in the illusion and how we have given it a reality it does not have.

The body is a fence the Son of God imagines he has built, to separate parts of his Self from other parts. It is within this fence he thinks he lives, to die as it decays and crumbles....And if he did not die, what 'proof' is there that God's eternal Son can be destroyed?...Made to be fearful, must the body serve the purpose given it. But we can change the purpose that the body will obey by changing what we think that it is for...The body is the means by which God's Son returns to sanity....The Son of God extends his hand to reach his brother, and to help him walk along the road with him. Now is the body holy.[2]

The ego's purpose for the body has been to confuse the dream with Reality, to keep us seeking out a small happiness here, or a little pleasure there, all the while keeping us engrossed in the dream of unforgiveness, forever chained to its precepts. The following excerpt outlines this problem.

Thus they define their life and where they live, adjusting to it as they think they must, afraid to lose the little that they have. And so it is with all who see the body as all they have and all their brothers have. They try to reach each other, and they fail, and fail again. And they adjust to loneliness, believing that to keep the body is to save the little that they have.[3]

We have truly ensconced ourselves in a perceptual prison, and have despairingly thought that there was no way out. The Holy Spirit's purpose for the body will become apparent as we remove the obstacles that have mired us in the ego's thought system, and He will help us surmount the precepts that have bound us. The Love that we are will shine forth and will not be hid. Jesus' words in *A Course in Miracles* comes to us as a ray of Light that touches our hearts with joy, for we discover the fact that we are forever beloved, and all of the destructive thoughts that we had believed about ourselves were untrue. The blindness that had dimmed our sight falls away and we see our brother as he is, and ourselves as we have always been.

As we now witness through forgiving eyes that we and our brother are the same and created in Love, we come to acknowledge only the everlasting One Spirit that resides within us all. By correctly using the body to return to sanity, we are bringing the dream to the Truth. Thus the body's purpose and goals becomes holy, and we can use it as vehicle for our redemption.

'Your safety lies in truth and not in lies. Love is your safety. Fear does not exist. Identify with love, and you are safe. Identify with love, and you are home. Identify with love, and find your Self.'[4]

If we keep in mind the previous discourse and take a closer look at the following Saying, we may see a new meaning that we might have overlooked.

87. J said, 'How miserable is the body that depends on a body, and how miserable is the soul that depends on these two.'

We find that this Saying parallels our discussions so far about the body consciousness. It recounts how we identify with our bodies, always looking outward for others to meet our varied psychological and physical needs. It is here that we project blame, self-justification and attack upon our brother, and we stay on the merry-go-round of the ego's world that is not merry at all.

These problems arose because we had mistakenly equated the body with the Self that God created. We have used the body to try to prove to ourselves that the world is real and not an effect (or symptom) of our Mind's decision to remain separate. The consequence of holding onto this idea of separation is to feel alone and abandoned. We feel bereft of the Unity that we so long for, but do not know where to look or how to find it.

The ego will call to us to seek here or there for some small happiness, and it always seems to remain just beyond reach. It is but a lure inside of a dream that has the intent of keeping us from seeking the only True Happiness that can only be found by rising above the thoughts of this world. Until we awaken, we will wander in and out of contrived circumstances and our soul will be miserable in its delusions and ever thirst for the Living Water of our Father's Kingdom that gives rest and peace everlasting.

In Saying 34 where Jesus speaks about the blind leading the blind, we see the inter-relatedness of these Sayings. Here we have blindly identified with our bodies and believe that we are seeing reality through the body's eyes. As we mentioned before, if we rely on our bodies to tell us what is true, we are asking for the truth from the one thing in the entire universe that doesn't know. (The ego thought construct does not, and cannot overlap in any way with the thoughts of Truth from the Holy Spirit.) We thereby give validity to the illusion and stay in the dream, never looking or believing that there is an escape, especially since we believe that the source of our problems occur outside of ourselves. The bodies and images that we see in the world bear no resemblance to our Self at all; those images were made to usurp our rightful reality as a Son of God.

As we absorb these teachings and are filled with their illumination, we shall come to recognize that everything that we perceive is occurring within our minds, and we do not see anything concrete outside of us at all. We are only seeing pictures in our minds, the same as we do when our eyes are closed. Now that we have this understanding, we will be able to see the problem as it is, not the way we have set it up to be.

Interestingly, if one set up debate teams where one side would try to prove the scientific physical reality of the world and the other side would challenge that idea, the scientific debate team would sorely lose. There is no demonstrable proof that anything that the senses see, feel, hear or touch is any more than a flurry of electrical charges interpreted by brain processes. Nor can it be verifiably argued that it is anything more than electrical bursts registering in the brain that gives us the impression that objects are solid to the touch or that light is transmitted to the eye. This means that it is impossible to verify a direct link between what registers in the cerebral cortex of our head and what we observe in the outside world. We do not observe this process because the flood of chemical nerve impulses happens so quickly that it instantaneously translates into what we perceive with our senses.[5] If we take our previous discussions into account, we can see how this explains how we are instantaneously manufacturing the world of perception around ourselves, and as an observer of the universe we are beyond time creating our world and all perceptions therein moment by moment.

Saying 87 reminds us just how miserable we are as we depend on, and believe in, the body's objectives, and how that path will only lead to more unhappiness. Let us recognize that our conviction as to who and what we are will follow in the direction of what we believe, and what we want. If we instruct our mind to accept once again that we are not a body but are the gossamer substance of Spirit in Whose Image we are created, we can escape the body consciousness to the extent that we desire to do so. The mistaken belief that we are the body is a belief to be undone, and we can call on the strength of our True Self and the Holy Spirit to bring to our awareness what is hidden by those mistaken convictions.

We need an *experience* of something Real to put our faith in, something more solid and sure to replace our faulty images. This is a wholly acceptable prayer that is our divine right as a Son of God to ask for and to receive. As we focus on our true Strength in God and merge with Him, we will recognize that any sense of weakness that we felt has come from identifying with this vulnerable body. We are resolved to remove our faith from that faulty identification and shift our focus toward a Divine Encounter.

We can ask ourselves; if we are not a body, then what are we? As we contemplate this question and allow our defective ego thoughts to fall away, we permit the Truth to replace the flawed concepts about who we are.

We are and could only be as God created us. We yearn to understand that we are not weak, but strong, we are not limited but limitless, and to know that who we truly are is not an illusion but a Reality. Since we cannot see anything that is Real in darkness but can only see what is meaningful in the Light, it is inevitable that as we grow in the Light that the darkness will dissipate and we will be able to accept the Truth of the Holy Spirit's dictates as our own.[6]

Our bodies, as all illusions, will fail us, as they are part of the misconception of what our Reality really is. The Holy Spirit's Vision is obscured by these dense concepts, and we remain trapped within the ego's desolate world. As we take the Holy Spirit's hand, it is by God's Grace that we see a glimmer of light to lead us out of the darkness. As we accept His guidance, we will find that even though we will see the same events as everyone else; our new perspective will be one of serenity, for the Holy Spirit has shown us the unreality of the ego's darkness. We have integrated His vision into ours and we see everything that occurs on this planet as Love or a call for Love.

We understand from Saying 87 that if we identify ourselves with the chimera body, our soul will be truly miserable and bereft. Since we are ensconced within the thought of form, we have deceived ourselves into depending on other mirages and dream figures to do certain things for us to be 'happy', but we have actually set ourselves up for disappointment in the short or long term. It is impossible for those images to live up to our expectations, because our ego self keeps drawing lines in the sand and lies in wait for them to fail us. If they don't fail us in the short term, we subconsciously keep changing the parameters until they do. To consider ourselves faultless, we convolutedly claim how we are the victims of circumstance, and feel justified in casting blame outwards deluding ourselves as to our own culpability. The following quote emphasizes how we entangle ourselves in made up thought constructs that inevitably backfire on us.

'Your insane laws were made to guarantee that you would make mistakes, and give them power over you by accepting their result as you just due.'[7]

The purpose of the ego's physical world was set up to fail and disappoint us. These insane laws were made to keep us entrenched in the ego's thought processes, where we are always trying to stay 'in line' but always failing in some measure. On the one hand, we try to follow these laws since they 'validate' the world's reality and substantiate our individuality, but on the other hand we find that we are wretched and don't know why. We can see how we have entrapped ourselves, but now more importantly, we can see how we can gain our freedom.

Jesus, in the Text of *A Course in Miracles* elaborates on these laws of chaos in depth. From our previous discussions we can garner some understanding of how these laws and other obstacles to our peace have been set up and operate in the world so that we will not fall as readily into the trap of ego minded thinking. We will now look at some additional ways that this buried secret dream erupts from our unconscious.

The Ego's Chaotic Laws
One of the wrong minded conceptual laws that we have already talked about is the belief that we are individually different, separate, or more special than our brother. That belief has come

from our projected comparisons and judgments about his form. Since form is an illusion of our own making, our misperceived interpretations will be rectified as we switch Teachers. The Holy Spirit will continually show us in every circumstance that we are the same in Spirit beyond form, and guilt will no longer need to be projected out because the separation of the One Son and consequently the guilt *has not happened*. We recognize that we as One are all beloved of our Father.

We have looked at our unwarranted fear of God and now understand that the multitudinous interactions that have taken place between ourselves and our brothers are nothing more than a product of the continuous subconscious reenactment of our formation story that seemed to put us at odds with our Father. All behaviors, concepts and interrelations that take place are a product of this destructive belief. Now we know that these are the thoughts that we must be vigilant for, and every time they surface to remember their origin and replace them with the Holy Spirit's thinking, which eternally proclaims the perpetual Love of our Father for His Son. All of our nightmares will be soothed away by a Loving Hand that gently maintains this foundational thought of our sinlessness beyond form.

We have not yet explored a significant obstacle to our attaining peace; the fear of the body's death. No matter how we try to rationalize our thoughts about death (nature taking its course, it is a part of life…) we subconsciously perceive that the death of our bodies and of those around us (as well as disease, maiming, accidents…) is a retribution for the act of betrayal and separation that was enacted by us against our Creator.

This is so if we consider that everything that happens in the world, and to us personally, is a dreaming reflection of the original moment of terror when we 'separated' from our Source. If we are identified with the body, this subliminal fear affects us all and cannot be denied, for even if death can be staved off for a time we must concede that it inexorably claims us all.

The world that we perceive reflects this fear of death by manifesting the demise of *everything* on this planet. It may take eons but eventually everything perishes, whether animate or inanimate. We cannot escape this reminder of death that continually surrounds us. Since we cannot hear the Voice that offers us a different account, we have accepted as true the ego's premise that we are physical and impermanent. This has left us ceaselessly terrified. Consequently, we secretly blame *and* fear this made-up vindictive God for our plight, and are thrown into a self-perpetuating nightmare from which there seems to be no escape.

Moreover, not only do we believe that we are persecuted by Him (evidenced by our body dying), but believe that the reason our lives are in perpetual turmoil is because we have done some 'terrible thing', or must be an 'awful person' and now 'God is getting us back.' To avoid these fearful thoughts we ensure that they are sublimated and projected out onto everybody (anybody) else, and then we have spent our lives trying to 'win' back the love and approval that was never lost in the first place. We can see how this concept has been reflected in our lives as we interrelate with others (our parents, our lovers, employers...). We have continually pointed out the faults of our brothers to deflect our own private sense of sin.

Further, somewhere in the mix of these confused perceptions we have tried to believe that God is loving, but as we survey this fearful, chaotic world of attack and death, we find that this idea of God's purported love is not consistent.

As we look at the world, there is a contradiction between the love that we should feel and the out-picturing of death and destruction that seems to surround us. In actuality, we have feared for our very lives, for we secretly believed that the chaos in the world was the manifestation of God's Will for our unforgivable transgressions.

We cry in travail over the fate of man who is subject to this punishing God, a God Who has allowed these tragedies to happen. We have shifted this underlying fear of our Father into our lives by believing if we do not walk a straight and narrow path, we would be punished in the near or distant future. When some calamity happens, we rely upon our ego mind to tell us what is true, and are told (predictably) that the adversity that befell us is deserved, and even though the world is clearly mad, there is no way out of its stifling confines. With that perception, we are plummeted into despair.

We have heard, and may believe in life after death, but this concept does not give much comfort, for we still perceive that God destroys the bodies that we have identified with. The thought of death sends shivers of fear to our very core. It is here within this thought construct that we need to take the Holy Spirit's hand, and let His Voice calm our tumultuous thoughts with the soothing assurance that our misperceptions are not so. We can see that this mindset that has caused us so much mental anguish could not be an aspect of our eternally Loving Father.

Now we can forgive ourselves for the troubles we have wrought and realize that this self-deceit was only a misperception of the source of our fears. We will take responsibility for the errors in our thinking and work to free ourselves of the deepseated beliefs in the falsehoods about ourselves. We will strive to have the *experience* of God's unequivocal and endless Love. That Love is only waiting for us to acknowledge its Presence to be released into our awareness.

In the following passages, Jesus kindly tells us of the errors in our thinking to bring us a reprieve from our mistaken thoughts.

The curious belief that there is a part (the soul) of dying things that may go on apart from what will die, (the body) does not proclaim a loving God nor re-establish any grounds for trust. If death is real for anything, there is no life. Death denies life. But if there is reality in life, death is denied. No compromise in this is possible. There is either a god of fear or One of Love.[8]

Here it is stated that the corruptible body that appears to die is not a part of our loving Father, for He is Life Eternal, and has no part in the dream of the dying and the lifeless. The Text of the *Course* goes on to relate:

The 'reality' of death is firmly rooted in the belief that God's Son is a body. And if God created bodies, death would indeed be real. But God would not be loving.[9]

This thought about the realities of death and the body, as well as many of the subjects discussed so far bears contemplation and much soul searching. The understanding of our previous discussions does not necessarily rely on acceptance of these aforementioned thoughts, but we may find that as we periodically revisit these ideas we will notice that they do prove consistent. We have seen that many of the Sayings from Thomas' Gospel sustain these ideas, along with Thomas' concealed parables that support the proposition that this 'desert' was not made by the Father, and that our 'tormentors' come from us. These perspectives are also in harmony with the much revered ancient Hindu philosophy of Vedanta. This philosophy has two primary tenets, one, that the innate nature of humanity is divine, and two, humanity's goal is to *realize* that their inherent nature is divine. (See Appendix C)

We must keep reminding ourselves that our bodies are not who we are, but we are as God created us and we are eternally One with Him. There is no other Reality but this loving Essence of which we are comprised. As it is God's Will, we *will* come to the awareness of the Divine, and the obstacles to peace that we have set up will dissolve.

God is your safety in every circumstance. His Voice (the Holy

Spirit) speaks for Him in all situations and in every aspect of all situations, telling you exactly what to do to call upon His strength and His protection. There are no exceptions because God has no exceptions.[10]

As we put our complete faith in the surety of God's everlasting Love we will always have the Answer to our prayers. We will get our answers in many ways, as an internal guidance, through dreams or from our brother who says the right thing at the right time. We are always answered, even though we can miss it, misunderstand it or even ignore it if the answer is not what we think it should be.

As the Lessons in the Workbook draw to a close, we find our inaccurate thought system is outlined, and our safety in God is summarized.

We are forgiven now. And we are saved from all the wrath we thought belonged to God, and found it was a dream. We are restored to sanity, in which we understand that anger is insane, attack is mad, and vengeance merely foolish fantasy. We have been saved from wrath because we learned we were mistaken. Nothing more than that. And is a father angry at his son because he failed to understand the truth?[11]

This excerpt dismisses all of the complexities of our mental mechanizations as irrelevant. With a great sense of relief, we are released from any importance that we had given our erroneous thoughts. We were only mistaken. We have found Peace and have come Home.

Chapter Five

A New Beginning

As we look at *A Course in Miracles* and correlate all of our source materials, we have come to see a recurring pattern. The message that has emerged and is repeated frequently is the Reality of our eternal Oneness, the Light within us that cannot be hid. We are so much more than we realize, and our purpose is to embrace our function of forgiveness and remove the blocks that we have placed between ourselves and the awareness of the Divine.

These materials point out in various ways the contrasts between our mistaken fear of annihilation, and the joyful news of the loving Presence of the Divine that has never left us. For this knowledge are we eternally grateful. To know our Father's unremitting Love is a balm that heals all hurts and mends all wounds.

The *Course* offers us many practical ways to embark on our spiritual journey. As we have pointed out, it is necessary to take the Holy Spirit's hand to guide us, as he will lead us through all of our mistaken interpretations and reveal the Truth as we continuously bring our illusions to Him throughout the day. As we know, the first thought to leap out into the forefront of our consciousness when we are confronted with an inflammatory situation is the ego's defensive thought system.

With this in mind, we can begin the work of training our minds to be aware of the dissonant thoughts as they come up. We should not struggle against them, for if we do, we only reinforce the idea that the discord is real. Instead, we *observe* the ego's projections, this being the process of looking within, and exchange the discordant thoughts for the Holy Spirit's vision that sees things very simply, as Love or a call for Love. As we look, we realize that our brother was a reflection of all that we did not want to confront in ourselves, and it is then that we can laugh at the mad idea that believed that we were outcasts and unloved. As we are vigilant in our efforts, we find that the hold that the ego had on us loosens, because we no longer sustain or protect it.

We have discussed the ego's thought system in depth and have come to an understanding that the ego has led us down a path of darkness that has kept us in the throes of insularity. We have made a world of darkness and have moved about in it thinking that we were seeing reality, but were actually groping blindly around with the faulty equipment that was made to insulate us from true vision.

We long for the Vision of the Holy Spirit that guides us to see clearly in the Light. As we move forward to attain Christic Vision, we must discipline our minds to see the Light that is beyond form. We may find that there is a remnant of fear that precludes us from entirely embracing the Holy Spirit's mindset because:

> ...you leave behind everything that you now believe, and all the thoughts that you have made up. Properly speaking, this is the release from hell. Yet perceived through the ego's eyes, it is loss of identity and a descent into hell.[1]

> We can overcome our fears by simply reminding ourselves, 'that to reach light is to escape from darkness, whatever you may believe to the contrary. God is the light in which you see. You are attempting to reach Him.'[2]

In the Workbook, Jesus gives us specific exercises to free our minds to see clearly. It would help us immeasurably if we used these exercises daily to quiet the jumbled commotion of our thinking. As we become aware of the holiness in which we practice we are propelled toward our *real* thoughts. Those holy thoughts found within our Mind are a part of the eternal Mind of

God. This is the only place Reality could be, because our thoughts have never left their Source.

We can take the Workbook lesson 'God is the light in which I see'[3], or any other that we find inspiring, and we repeat it slowly, and close our eyes to go deeply into our minds. We drop our awareness below the senseless chatter of the ego mind that tries to cover the Truth and divert our attention. Our objective is to let go of all of the interference that would try to block our advance, and attempt a holy exercise to reach the Thoughts of God that we had with Him in the beginning.

We can ascertain our progress by a sensation of relaxation, and '...a feeling that you are approaching, if not actually entering into light. Try to think of light, formless and without limit, as you pass by the thoughts of this world. And do not forget that they cannot hold you to the world unless you give them the power to do so.'[4]

If our mind wanders, let us gently bring it back to the pure thought-form with which we began. Sooner or later we will be successful, and even first attempts may have very surprising results. Ultimately we cannot fail, for our will is now in accord with God's Will as we reverently touch the hem of His garment.

Throughout our varied discussions of these texts, we have seen the consistent threads running through them and have attempted to knit them together. As a lot of these thoughts are new to us, our task becomes to take this newly acquired knowledge and make it our own and transform our learning into becoming.

It will take continuous application and concentration to yield the rewards that transcend the world. We therefore need to delve within to find the Truth of these Sayings and teachings for ourselves. By doing so we can then; 'remove all projections of guilt from our brother, (and it will) express the vision of Christ that sees all united in the Sonship of God. This vision looks beyond the seeming differences that reflect separation to the (light beyond the form and the) recognition that (we are whole in God.) What we thought was done to us we did to ourselves... (It is) then we will come to a true understanding of forgiveness and the peace of God.'[5] We will have then shifted our perception to see everything in union with God.

Hence, 'we return' to the perfection of God's Peace because our minds are joined, and Love flows from one to another unhindered by imaginary obstructions. We will find that implementation of these teachings can change our view of a tired world to one that sparkles with promise.

As we lay down our dreams of hatred and attack and choose forgiveness as a way of life, we will come to the understanding of who we are in reality. As Jesus says in the Text;

Accept the dream He gave instead of yours. It is not difficult to change a dream when once the dreamer has been recognized. Rest in the Holy Spirit...His gentle dreams take the place of those you dreamed in terror and in fear of death. He brings forgiving dreams, (where) there is no murder and there is no death. The dream of guilt is fading from your sight, although your eyes are closed....Dream softly of your sinless brother, who unites with you in holy innocence. And from this dream the Lord of Heaven will Himself awaken His beloved Son. Dream of your brother's kindnesses instead of dwelling in your dreams on his mistakes....Forgive him his illusions...And do not brush aside his many gifts because he is not perfect in you dreams.[6]

As we become permeated with the Light of our Real Self, the Light extends to our brothers calling them Home. They see in that Light their own their own holiness, and thereby know their sins are the forgiven mistakes that never were. Jesus reminds us of our eternal Divinity:

You are a child of God, a priceless part of His Kingdom, which He created as part of Him. Nothing else exists and only this is real. You have chosen a sleep in which you have had bad dreams, but the sleep is not real and God calls you to awake.[7]

Let us remember that there is no division in God's Kingdom, and the Son rests as One in eternal timelessness and *everything* else is a product of the dream.

God does not suffer conflict. Nor is His creation split in two. How could it be His Son could be in hell, when God Himself established him in Heaven?[8]

No, we no longer believe in the dream as fervently, and we now endeavor to replace the fearful thoughts that we had made with the shining Thoughts of our Father. As the futile thoughts of the ego fade away, our awareness of the Divine is restored to us from the safety of the Holy Spirit's thought system where it always has resided. Our Birthright has only been waiting in quiet anticipation for us to accept it back into our awareness.

Chapter Six

An Ancient Memory Reborn

As the obstacles to the recognition of the Divine fade away and we can once again hear our Father's Voice, our love and gratitude knows no bounds and rises to Heaven wafting a fragrance so lovely as to enchant the angels.

Now we hear a distant melody calling that is somehow familiar. As we curiously turn to find the source of this ancient hymn, we see in our mind's eye a beautiful door that we know has been long shut. The melody comes from beyond it. This is the door that beckons us, this is the door that bespeaks of Truth, this is the door that we desire; all worldly temptations fade before the summoning call from beyond its entrance. Finally, after a lifetime of struggle and strife, the key is in our hand and we are ready to open this door that leads to the ending of all dreams and is the gateway to Heaven. This is the entrance which we have never forgotten and have eternally sought.

Let us wait no longer in uncertainty, let us forgive all things, and let creation be as our Father would have it be and as it is. Let us remember that we are our Father's Son, and as we turn the key, we find the door swings open easily, for our touch is sure, our objective clear. As we walk in forgiveness with our brother at our side, His memory returns to us and we forget all of our illusions in the blazing light of Truth.[1]

As this door is opened, the joyful tidings of our return are trumpeted throughout Heaven, and we find, 'Angels light the way, so that all darkness vanishes, and you are standing in a light so bright and clear that you can understand all things you see...you realize the world you see before you in the light reflects the truth you knew, and did not quite forget in wandering away in dreams.'[2] Here is the vision of the Son's aspirations come true.

As we consider these passages, let us reflect upon our eternal Oneness with our Creator. We seek to experience the Reality of the Christic Mind that knows that He has never left his Source. The Holy Spirit and the Angels beckon for us to step through this ancient doorway that gently welcomes us as it opens to reveal the Truth of our One Self.

Beyond the body, beyond the sun and stars, past everything you see and yet somehow familiar, is an arc of golden light that stretches as you look into a great and shining circle. And all the circle fills with light before your eyes. The edges of the circle disappear, and what is in it is no longer contained at all. The light expands and covers everything, extending to infinity forever shining and with no break or limit anywhere. Within it everything is joined in perfect continuity. Nor is it possible to imagine that anything could be outside, for there is nowhere that this light is not.

This is the vision of the Son of God, whom you know well. Here is the sight of him who knows his Father. Here is the memory of what you are; a part of this, with all of it within, and joined to all as surely as all is joined in you. Accept the vision that can show you this, and not the body. You know the ancient song, an ancient hymn of love the Son of God sings to his Father still.

What is a miracle but this remembering? And who is there in whom this memory lies not? The light in one awakens it in all.[3]

Acknowledgements

I would like to express my deepest gratitude, first and foremost to Jesus for the gift of A Course in Miracles. His love is continually expressed throughout these pages assuring us that we are never alone but always tenderly watched over and gently guided. The light and love have leaped off the pages reaching into the darkest corners of my consciousness illuminating the road that we all must travel back to the beginning so that we may know the end. This document opened my eyes to a world beyond the farthest reaches of my imagination and by the Grace of God has set the direction of my compass pointing Home. I am eternally indebted to Helen Schucman for being open to receive this message of Living Light and to Bill Thetford for his encouragement and help in transcribing these teachings.

I also want to express appreciation to Gary R. Renard for his uncompromising determination to take down the message of Arten and Pursah. His books have catapulted my understanding to a new level, and has enhanced my understanding of the underlying meaning and message of the Course.

My sincerest thanks to Dr. Kenneth Wapnick for his comprehensive work of disseminating the teachings of A Course in Miracles. His in-depth understanding of these timeless teachings has assisted my comprehension immeasurably. His efforts are far reaching and will undoubtedly traverse the ages.

Appendix A

The Gnostic Society Library
The Gospel of Thomas Collection
The Greek Oxyrhynchus Fragments

In 1897 and 1903 three ancient fragments from Greek versions of the *Gospel of Thomas* were discovered during archeological excavations on the site of an ancient library at Oxyrhynchus, Egypt (a project that eventually recovered over 5000 fragments of ancient Greek texts once present in the library). The three papyrus fragments of Thomas apparently date to between 130 - 250 CE, and each probably represents a separate unique copy of the Gospel. The textual source of the sayings contained in the fragments was initially unclear; based on the logion found in pOxy 654 – now identified as containing the prologue and first saying – it was speculated they might represent remains of the lost *Gospel of Thomas*. The Nag Hammadi discovery in 1945 which unearthed a complete and well-preserved version of Thomas in Coptic made it possible to definitely identify the Oxyrhynchus texts as fragments from a lost Greek edition of the Gospel.

This website includes remnants of Oxyrhynchus fragments for our review from logion 26 to 30, 77, and 30 to 31; also the pOxy 654 remnants contains logion 1 to 7; and pOxy 655 preserves logion 36 to 40. These texts allow careful comparisons to be made between the Coptic text found at Nag Hammadi and the original Greek version (the Gospel was almost certainly written in Greek originally, the Nag Hammadi version is a Coptic translation of this original Greek text). The reader will note close correlation between the two versions – a fact that helps verify the textual integrity of the Coptic *Gospel of Thomas*.

In summation, at this website we will find translations of the Greek Oxyrhynchus fragments, followed by versions of the same sayings as they appear in the *Gospel of Thomas* Coptic text that were found at Nag Hammadi.

Appendix B

Jesus and Aramaic

Jesus' spoke *Aramaic*, the common language of Galilee during his lifetime. Aramaic was an ancient Semitic language related to Hebrew much as French is related to Spanish or as Cantonese is related to Mandarin. (Thanks to Prof. Zev bar-Lev for help with these analogies.) Though Jews had once spoken Hebrew as their primary language, this changed when Israel was overthrown, first by the Assyrians in the eight-century B.C. and then by the Babylonians in the sixth-century B.C. By the time of Jesus Aramaic was so common among Jews that the reading of the Hebrew Scripture in the synagogue was accompanied by translation into Aramaic. (For a helpful overview of Aramaic, see the 'Comprehensive Aramaic Lexicon' website of Hebrew Union College.) In addition to the strong circumstantial evidence that Jesus spoke Aramaic as his primary luuage, we can find direct evidence for this theory from the New Testament gospels. Though these gospels were written originally in Greek, at several points Jesus' words are given in Aramaic, for example: *'Talitha cum'* (Mark 5:41, 'Little girl, get up!'); 'Abba' (Mark 14:36. 'Father'); *'Eloi, Eloi, lema sabachtani?'* (Mark 15:34, 'My God, my God, why have you forsaken me?'). In these cases the actual Aramaic words of Jesus were remembered and passed on even by Greek-speaking Christians.

These passages and others from the gospels, combined with the predominance of Aramaic in Palestine in the first century A.D., make it virtually certain that Aramaic was Jesus' primary language. (There are a few scholars who believe that Hebrew was the primary language of Jesus, but they are quite in the minority. See, for an example, the Jerusalem School of Synoptic Research.)

Jesus Revealed: Rev. Dr. Mark D. Roberts

Appendix C

Advaita Vedanta

All forms of Hindu Vedanta are drawn primarily from a set of philosophical and instructive Vedic scriptures named the Upanishads.

Advaita Vedānta was propounded by Adi Sankara and his grand-guru Gaudapada. The definition of advaita is 'non-duality'. According to this school of Vedānta, Brahman is the only reality, and the world, as it appears, is illusory. Since Brahman is the sole reality, the world cannot be said to possess any attributes whatsoever. Therefore, an illusionary power of Brahman called Māyā causes the world as we see it to arise. Our ignorance of the illusory reality of this world is the cause of all suffering and only when the true knowledge of Brahman is attained can liberation be achieved.

When a person tries to know Brahman through his mind and strives to attain enlightenment, because of the influence of Māyā, Brahman can't be seen as the sole reality, so He is perceived as God (Ishvara), and is seen as separate from the world and from the individual. But in reality, there is no difference between the individual soul (= Atman) and Brahman. Liberation lies in knowing the reality of this non-difference. Thus, the path to liberation is finally only through knowledge.

Wikipedia.com, the free encyclopedia

Appendix D

This ancient Coptic language text found near Nag Hammadi is the only complete copy of *Thomas' Gospel* in existence. Since the common spoken language at the time of Thomas and Jesus was Aramaic (see Appendix B), one can surmise that all original writings in that language must have been destroyed, but not before they were mistranslated, copied, recopied, or added to, leaving us only with an altered version in a different language. As we mentioned previously, the Greek Oxyrhynchus fragments significantly predate and differ from this ancient Coptic text (See Appendix A) and lend credence to these statements of alteration.

These Sayings have been revised but some are edited for accuracy and certain Sayings are omitted altogether as not being the words of the Master. Moreover, as Saying 6 and 14 got mixed up over the years that this document was in circulation, these two Sayings were combined in this rendition.

Additionally, even though numbers for the Sayings did not originally exist in the text and were added later, we have kept the Nag Hammadi Text's numbering system the same for clarity and reference, and these are the numbers we refer to as we discuss various Sayings. The numbers 1-70 are added in parenthesis to provide a numbering system for Pursah's document, to make a total of 70 corrected Sayings, as compared to the original 114 in the Nag Hammadi Text.

Footnote References

Part I

Origins

(1) *The Secret Sayings of Jesus,* Robert M. Grant, pg. 64 (2) The Coptic language is a now an unused ancient Egyptian dialect (3) Mark 4:11 (4) Mark 4:34 (5) *Your Immortal Reality;* Gary Renard, pgs.162-171(6) Author of *Disappearance of the Universe* and *Your Immortal Reality*

A Course in Miracles

(1) Job.33:4 (2) John.14:10 (3) John.14:12 (3A) W323.5:1-7 (4) *I Am That,* Sri Nisargadatta Maharaj, Pg. 292 (5) W23.1:2-5 (6) W434, Lesson 276 (7) W431.1:1-3; 4:1 (8) ACIM.Preface; vii, viii (9) DU 82

The Ego

(1) M81-82.1:5-6;8:1 (2) W63.3:1-2 (3) W467.1:l, 2:2 (4) W467.4:1;3:1,4

Unfolding Insights

(1) Romans7:19 (2) Shankara, *Crest Jewel of Discrimination,* pgs. 7, 8, 9, 13, 14 (3) Plato, *The Republic* (4) T586.6:2 (5) W190.2:1 (6) T409.6:8 (7) W473.4:1-3

The Perception of Sin

(1) Random House Webster's College Dictionary (2) T656.1:1-2,5-7;2:2-3

A Discourse on Judgment

(1) W278.1:1-4 (2) W279.7:2-4 (3) T587.9:2-5 (4) *The Holographic Universe,* Michael Talbot pg. 1 (5) T648.12:1-4;13:1-5 (6) W25.1:1-7 (7) T409.9:6 (8) T478.1:1-4, 7; T479.3:10-12 (9) M26.2:4

The Dream

(1) DU 112 (2) DU 291 (3) W18.1:2-4 (4) T473.10:1-2 (5) T479.5:2-4
(6) T480.6:8 (7) T554.6:7-10 (8) T388.h (8A) *Glossary of Terms from
A Course in Miracles*, Robert Perry, pg.56 (9) W245.h

Forgiveness

(1) W401.1:1-4; 2:1 (2) preface xiii (3) W416.Lesson 246 (4)
Mark.12:28-31 (5) W281.5:1-2 (6) T354.6:1-2 (7) W443.1:4, 2:5-6 (8)
DU 171 (9) W197.h (10) T601.3:1 (11) T600.10:1 (12) DU 235-240
(13) T93.7:1 (14) W479.1:1-6 (15) W439.Lesson 284 (16) T512.7:1-3;
8:7-8

The Double Shield

(1) T584.12:3-6 (2) *Don Quixote* had no doubt that as he charged
windmills that he was going into battle with ferocious giants. (3)
T585.16:2 (4) *Dreaming the Dream*, CD Collection (5) T55.9:1-4, 6;
8:6-7 (6) T148.4:1 (7) Preface. x (8) Preface. xiii (9) W407.3:1-3 (10)
T638.1:1-4 (11) W366.9:2-5

Part 2

Preamble to the Gospel

(1) See Saying 22 (2) Phil.4:7

Libretto

(2) W415.Lesson 243 (3) T381.4:2 (4) G-I.173, *(italics mine)* (5)
T235.8:1,3 (6) M52.5:7-8, 10 (7) M68.3:3; 1:10 (8) M67.6:10 (9)
T448.2:1-7 (10) T351.2:4, 4:3-4, T352.6:2 (11) T472.4:4-6 (12) Matt.
6:24 (13) T515.4:8 (14) W458. Lesson 315 (15) T13.5:1-4,7 (16)
T112.2:8 (17) G-I.40 (18) M67.7:3-5 (19) T599.7:1-2; T392.8:1-3 (20)
T380.8:7; G-I.89 (21) T359.9:1-5 (22) W235.1:3 (23) W443.4:2 (24)
W357.1:1-3 (25) T98.12:3, 5, 8 (26) W245.h (27) T587.10:1-4 (28)
W284.3:2 (29) G-I.72 (30) G-I.137 (31) T555.9:1-2,5 (32) T554.4:8-9
(33) W451.Lesson304 (34) T445.1:1-2,5-9 (35) T349.9:2-6 (36)
W217.1:1-6;2:1;4:1 (37) W217.3:1-2 (38) DU 264 (39) John 16:33

(40) T446.2:5 (41) T446.4:1-7 (42) W300.5:3-4 (43) T98.10:7 (44) Matt.6:22 (45) T496.6:1-7 (46) W294.2:4-5 (47) W67.3:2 (48) T117.5:1 (49) T575.4:4-9,16;5:6-8 (50) W299.7:1-5; 9:3 (51) T617.1:9 (52) W291.4:2-4; 5:1 (53) T384.1:5-6 (54) T384.1:1-2 (55) T54.7:6,8-9 (56) T562.1:5-6 (57) T117.3:5-6 (58) T617.1:9 (59) DU 27 (60) T25.1:6-7 (61) W293.12:4 (62) W307.h (63) W307.2:4-6 (64) Shankara's Crest-Jewel of Discrimination, Pg. 98 (65) T396.11:4 (65A) T51,paraphrased (66) T194.2:1,3,6

Three Enigmatic Parables
(1) Portion of Saying 13, or PGT 10 (1A) DU 81 (2) *Psychotherapy: Purpose, Process and Practice, pg. 15* (3) W443.2:1,6;3:4 (4) T554-5.6:7-10

The Body's Function
(1) DU 143 (2) W425.1:1-3, 2:9, 3:4-5, 4:1,3-4 (3) T446.5:1-4 (4) W425.5:3-8 (5) *The Book of Secrets*, Deepak Chopra, pg.20,21,paraphrased (6)W157, paraphrased (7) T432.3:1 (8) M66.4:1-6 (9) M67.5:1-3 (10) W75.3:1-3 (11) W485.5:2-7

A New Beginning
(1) W69.5:4-6 (2) W69.6:2-3 (3) W69.h (4) W70.10:1-3 (5) G-I.72 (6) T584.14:1-6; T585.15:1-6 (7) T101.6:1-3 (8) W240.8:1-3

An Ancient Memory Reborn
(1) W474.Lesson 342 (2) W241.13:2-3 (3) T447.9:1-6; 10:4-5

Bibliography

A Course in Miracles; 2nd Edition

Disappearance of the Universe; Gary R. Renard, Hay House, 2002, 2003, 2004

Your Immortal Reality; Gary R. Renard, Hay House, 2006

The Nag Hammadi Library; James M. Robinson, General Editor

Song of Prayer; Foundation for Inner Peace

Psychotherapy: Purpose, Process and Practice; Foundation for Inner Peace

Absence from Felicity; Dr. Ken Wapnick, PhD, Foundation for Inner Peace

A Vast Illusion; Dr. Ken Wapnick, PhD, Foundation for Inner Peace

Forgiveness and Jesus; Dr. Ken Wapnick, PhD Foundation for Inner Peace

Glossary-Index, 6th Edition; Dr. Ken Wapnick, PhD Foundation for Inner Peace

Glossary of Terms from A Course in Miracles; Robert Perry, Circle Publishing, 2nd Edition, 1996, 2005

Living a Course in Miracles; Dr. Kenneth Wapnick, PhD, Nightingale Press, CD Collection, Foundation for Inner Peace

Dreaming the Dream; Dr. Kenneth Wapnick, PhD, Workshop on CD, Foundation for Inner Peace

Shankara's Crest Jewel of Discrimination; Swami Prabhavananda and Christopher Isherwood

The Holographic Universe, Michael Talbot, HarperPerennial, 1991

The Book of Secrets, Deepak Chopra, Three Rivers Press, 2004

I Am That, Sri Nisargadatta Maharaj, The Acorn Press, 1973

The Republic; Plato, Oxford World's Classics

Don Quixote; Miguel de Cervantes, Penguin Classics

The Gnostic Society Library; wwwThe Gospel of Thomas: Oxyrhynchus Fragments, (Appendix A)

Jesus Revealed; Rev. Dr. Mark. D. Roberts, WaterbrookPress, 2002
    (Appendix B)
The Secret Sayings of Jesus; Robert M. Grant, Penguin Books, 1960
The King James Version Bible; KJV

BOOKS

O is a symbol of the world, of oneness and unity. In different cultures it also means the "eye," symbolizing knowledge and insight. We aim to publish books that are accessible, constructive and that challenge accepted opinion, both that of academia and the "moral majority."

Our books are available in all good English language bookstores worldwide. If you don't see the book on the shelves ask the bookstore to order it for you, quoting the ISBN number and title. Alternatively you can order online (all major online retail sites carry our titles) or contact the distributor in the relevant country, listed on the copyright page.

See our website **www.o-books.net** for a full list of over 500 titles, growing by 100 a year.

And tune in to myspiritradio.com for our book review radio show, hosted by June-Elleni Laine, where you can listen to the authors discussing their books.